Table of Contents

Preface   vii

Part I: Developing Visions, Creating Infrastructures

Childhood's End: Visions of the Internet   3
*Rosemarie E. Falanga, Director, Library and
Information Services. Exploratorium, San Francisco,
California*

School Instructional Information Managers:
    Leading the Way Today to Tomorrow   15
*Nina Little, Supervisor of Library and Instructional
Information Services. Omaha Public Schools, Omaha,
Nebraska*

A "Newbie" Asks   23
*Dale E. Beasley, Teacher. St. Philomena School, Des
Moines, Washington*

Following the Internet Highway in the Sciences   35
*Barry E. Rowe, Director of Educational Technology.
Champaign Unit #4 Schools, Champaign, Illinois*

A Statewide preK-12 Model for Internet Connectivity   43
*Wayne Fisher, Internet Specialist. Education Technology
Center, Nebraska Department of Education*

Part II: Building Models

Internet Infusion Models: Uses of the Internet in
    a Suburban K-12 Public School District   55
*Donald E. Jacobsen, Technology Support Specialist.
Millard Public Schools, Omaha, Nebraska*

Internet Access and Curricular Use in Wisconsin
   Schools   65
*Neah J. Lohr, Consultant. Microcomputer and
Instructional Technology, Wisconsin Department
of Public Instruction, Madison, Wisconsin*

Education on the Info Highway: The Nueva School,
   NuevaNet, and PIPE   75
*Ray Olszewski, Computer Systems Specialist.
The Nueva School, Hillsborough, California*

Boulder Valley Internet Projects   89
*John R. Speckien, Project Coordinator, Creating
Connections. Boulder Valley School District,
Boulder, Colorado*

Telecomputing in Smart Schools   97
*Dr. Charles Stallard. Hampton City Schools,
Hampton, Virginia*

Part III: Integrating the Internet with Curriculum

Nine Rules for Using the Internet in Class   107
*David Bell, Teacher. Louisville Junior High School.
Louisville, Nebraska*

Net Gain: Internet Use at New Vista High School   117
*Stevan Kalmon, Teacher. New Vista High School,
Boulder, Colorado*

Jazz Up your Curriculum with Global SchoolNet
   Telecommunications Projects   127
*Lorna Pasos, Project Coordinator. Global SchoolNet
Foundation, El Cajon, California*

Surfing the Internet in Santa Cruz   135
*Jory Post, Teacher. Happy Valley School,
Santa Cruz, California*

Part IV: Publishing on the Web

Vocal Point: A Collaborative, Student Run
   Online Newspaper   147
*Scott Dixon, Teacher, Centennial Middle School,
and Libby Black, Director, Boulder Valley Internet
Project. Boulder, Colorado*

THE
INTERNET
FOR
TEACHERS AND SCHOOL
LIBRARY MEDIA SPECIALISTS

TODAY'S APPLICATIONS
TOMORROW'S PROSPECTS

EDWARD J. VALAUSKAS AND MONICA ERTEL

NEAL-SCHUMAN NETGUIDE SERIES

 **Neal-Schuman Publishers, Inc.**
New York   London

Published by Neal-Schuman Publishers, Inc.
100 Varick Street
New York, NY 10013

Printed and bound in the United States of America

Library of Congress Cataloging-in-Publication Data

The Internet for teachers and school library media specialists :
    today's applications, tomorrow's prospects / edited by Edward J.
    Valauskas and Monica Ertel.
        p.   cm.
    Includes bibliographical references and index.
    ISBN 1–55570–239–2 (alk. paper)
    1. Education—Computer network resources. 2. Teaching—
Computer network resources. 3. Internet (Computer network)
I. Valauskas, Edward. II. Ertel, Monica.
LB1044.87.I58   1996
370'.285—dc20   96–2318

Interactive Internet; or, How Your School can
   Publish on the World Wide Web   159
Curtis Jensen. Area Education Agency 7, Cedar
Falls, Iowa

Constructing Educational Web Pages: Moving
   Beyond "Show and Tell"   169
Caroline McCullen, Teacher. Ligon GT Magnet
Middle School, Raleigh, North Carolina

Imagine the Possibilities: Exploring the Internet
   with Middle School Students   181
Barbara Spitz, Integration Specialist, Instructional
Technologies. Madison Metropolitan School District,
Madison, Wisconsin

Part V: Postscript

Learning with the Internet: Prospects for Tomorrow   195
Kim Rose. Apple Computer, Inc., Learning Concepts Group

Part VI: Appendices

Bibliography   205
Internet Sites Mentioned in this Book   209
Interesting Web Sites   215
Index   225
About the Editors   233

Preface

The Internet is changing the business of education. It is changing the relationships between student and teacher, parent and school, and administrator and voter. The process by which children learn about their world is changing drastically. No longer will memorization and factual accumulation count for as much as in the past. Creativity, evaluative skills, and digital diplomacy have become crucial in learning, for both the instructors and students.

With the Internet, introspective students can work on a level playing field with more aggressive and socially adept students. Being technologically adept has indeed become a status to strive for among the young. With the Internet, it does not matter what you look like, how you talk, or what you wear. Ideas are the currency of the networks and ideas have more value in this medium than any material or physical association. The rise in the value of ideas makes education fun and exciting, not a tedious task to pass the time. Both the young and adults are energized by this medium in a way never possible before.

A recent *USA Today*[1] article stated that "There's going to be a time, two or three years down the road, if your school's not connected, you're not providing an education." The connection being referred to is, of course, the Internet—the world's largest computer network. Schools are already connecting at a rapid rate. According to the same *USA Today* article, in October of 1995, more than 1200 elementary and secondary schools worldwide had Web pages on the Internet, up from just fifty a year ago. If you have access to the World Wide Web, you can find direct links to most of these sites at http:// web66.coled.umn.edu/schools.html—the Web66: International WWW School Registry.

The Internet for Teachers and School Library Media Specialists is an original collection of success stories. It is written by teachers, media specialists, and school administrators who have developed their own programs and facilities to bring the Internet to their students. Our goal was to produce a book which would inspire and educate teachers and school librarians interested in making the most of this amazing new educational tool. In this book, teachers and librarians discuss the pitfalls and success stories of getting kids on the Internet. You will find here explanations about how innovative projects such as the *MidLink Magazine* were created, as well as descriptions of specific lesson plans using the Internet. You will also read about setting up Internet programs in rural as well as urban schools. Future scenarios for Internet usage in schools are also described. The uses of the Internet are as varied as the people who use it.

Funding for Internet projects can come from a variety of sources. The projects in this book illustrate a handful of ways that money and resources can be found to finance a school's Internet presence and usage. While some lucky schools were able to get funding from their administrations, others were also able to fund their projects through partnerships with local universities and businesses, while some were able to obtain grants and others solicited support through donations. The key is to be creative as well as relentless in your pursuit for sources to get your school on the information superhighway.

This book's four main parts parallel the stages educators progress through when incorporating the Internet into the instructional process.

Part I, "Developing Visions, Creating Infrastructures," opens with a vision of what the Internet offers learners and its possibilities for opening minds and expanding horizons. This is followed by three tried-and-true plans for creating infrastructures for accessing and using the Internet. These include funding, staffing, and hardware components.

Part II, "Building Models," looks at the Internet as one part of the total educational technology picture. This section of the book features five "success stories" that describe how individual schools and school districts advanced from a desire to use the Internet to actually applying it, by training faculty and students alike and involving it in classroom instruction.

Part III, "Integrating the Internet with the Curriculum," is an especially crucial part of the book for today's educational scene. Just as integrating media skills and writing into and across the curriculum have been important educational goals for many years, integrating Internet skills into the curriculum is already being recognized as a major factor in effective instruction. The four descriptions included here offer both models and inspiration.

Part IV, "Publishing on the Web," discusses both the technical and educational aspects of Web publishing in schools. From surveys to newspapers, the innovative educational projects described in this part of the book are truly ground-breaking.

In the Postscript, "Learning with the Internet: Prospects for Tomorrow," Apple Computer's Kim Rose looks at the educational environment, computer literacy, and virtual communities as crucial interrelated elements of an increasingly technologically-driven world. Her insights can help today's teachers educate tomorrow's achievers.

In addition to the chapters by teachers and media specialists and the Postscript, we have also included several useful appendices including a list of the Internet sites referenced in this book, a list of additional educational Internet sites, and a bibliography of books.

These essays, stories, and reports from the Internet front in schools around the United States are inspiring tales of discipline and struggle to bring the Internet into the schools. They are only a sample of the possibilities, but they point to a future in education unlike anything we can imagine. What will these Internet-savvy youngsters do in the classroom when they become the principals? What will they do when they occupy the governor's office or chair the board of education? How will they react as the chief executives of telecommunications companies and software operations? The efforts by technologically fearless educators in this generation will bear fruit long into the next century and beyond. It has been an exciting journey thus far—and the odyssey has just begun.

As a final note, this entire book was planned using the Internet. We found the authors of the chapters inside this book by scouting the Internet for interesting projects, we contacted the authors via the Internet, and we communicated throughout the production process with these authors and our publisher over the Internet. When you're done reading, ideas for your own projects will come to mind. Some of these project ideas will be small while others will be larger and more ambitious. But to get started, do as our contributors did. Jump in and start to explore what's out there. Don't be afraid to ask questions. Look at what other schools have done and borrow their ideas. In turn, offer your ideas back to others. We're all learners in this adventure.

Edward J. Valauskas
g0094@applelink.apple.com

Monica Ertel
ertel.m@applelink.apple.com

NOTES

1.   Nicole Carroll, "Schools stake out spots in cyberspace," *USA Today*, October 9, 1995, p. 1D.

2.   Based on a report by the U. S. Department of Education, and discussed in Carla Schutte, "Survey finds most students with little access to Internet," *cy.Rev: A Journal of Cybernetic Revolution, Sustainable Socialism and Radical Democracy*, #3 (October 1995), pp. 22-23.

Part I:

Developing Visions, Creating Infrastructures

Childhood's End:
Visions of the Internet

Rosemarie E. Falanga
Director, Library and Information Services
Exploratorium
San Francisco, California

Overview—The Numbers	
Name of School, District or State:	Exploratorium San Francisco, CA
Number of teachers:	6 Library staff and 300 Museum staff
Number of students:	Serve 2,500 teachers as a teacher resource center
Grades covered:	K-12 teachers
Amount of money in grant or special expenditure (if applicable): n/a	

ABSTRACT

The Internet is not just mainframe relays; it is not just high-speed bandwidth; it is not just multimedia-ready personal computers. The Internet is people. It starts with people and ends with them. Through stories about children, real and imagined, this essay explores the role that the Internet plays in our lives both as it exists and as it might be. These stories provide a means to imagine the potential of the Internet as a way to change the way we learn and the way we live.

INTRODUCTION

An increasing number of Internet users are children. They are the real backbone and the real future of this network of computers and people. In order to make it possible to internalize a sense of the Internet as it is and as it might be, I will tell two stories about children, real and imagined, and the role that the Internet might play in their lives.

We all know these children; they have come to us over the years, in the classroom, across the library desk. Their stories are not new. We have done our best to help them and frequently succeeded. Now we have a new tool with which to help them, the Internet.

The following two scenarios portray these children. Each scenario is then followed by a discussion relating the child's interests, needs, and abilities to the new and expanded learning environment the Internet enables us to offer.

SCENARIO ONE: GREAT EXPECTATIONS

George's family was happy and well-balanced; everyone said so. The parents were both educated professionals; they were devoted to their children. The mother had delayed her career to stay home with the children while they were young. The family did things together and all three children had active school and social lives. They were enrolled in the best elementary schools, even when it meant the family had to move to another town to have access to a better school system. Their free time was divided between chess, cheerleading, football, and scouting. Everything was normal. Their parents put away money that would guarantee education through graduate school in any career they chose.

But as George approached adolescence, something began to go wrong. His active imagination, so charming in a young child, blossomed into a mania for fantasy. He devoured sword and sorcery books and comics. He would regale even casual visitors with elaborate stories that he made up as he went along endlessly. It was hard to tell if he believed that the stories actually happened or not.

He especially loved fantasy games on the computer. His father had brought an older model home so that all the children could learn word processing and turn out better homework. But George dominated its usage, pushing his siblings away psychically and sometimes physically.

At times the scene around the computer resembled a bunch of baby birds, too big and too many for the nest, arguing over who gets the worm. One way or another, George always got the biggest piece.

One day he came home, not with a kitten or a puppy trailing behind, but with a modem and a rudimentary telecommunications program. The battles escalated, since he was now frequently head-to-head with his parents over who controlled the phone. He would rise early in order to be alone with the computer, run home after school, and rush through his homework and dinner in order to squeeze an extra twenty minutes online.

He dialed up local bulletin boards on any and every topic. He spent almost his entire allowance on games and computer books. He discontinued his former extracurricular activities and friendships and began to develop e-mail relationships with others who had similar interests. His electronic companions taught him how to do neat things with his computer: how to download software and graphics and how to write simple programs. They instructed him in the ways to dial into computers with poor security systems. Soon he was accessing his school's computer and messing around with its files and records. He also took to hanging around the local library's computer lab, trying out software programs borrowed from his friends. His experimentation crashed the network several times, so he was forbidden to use it anymore.

His parents didn't understand what he was doing, and they were bewildered and frequently angry about the behavior they observed. "If only he would be more normal," they complained, "and play outside once in a while or have a friend over. If only he would read real books and have regular interests like his brother and sister. We were never like this when we were children." They considered forcing him to spend an hour outdoors for every hour he spent online. They considered getting rid of the computer. They considered taking him to a psychiatrist.

In the end they did none of these things. George continued on, barely getting by in school, becoming more and more estranged from his family and most of his teachers and schoolmates. The only way in which he grew intellectually was by acquiring a fine ability to make computers run, both through hardware and software configuration and through programming. As he grew older, he began picking up odd programming jobs. He began to see a way to earn a living by doing what he enjoyed. His battles with his parents became fierce. As soon as he finished high school, he left home to live with one of his hacker buddies. Now, in his late twenties, he makes a decent living and gets to work on sophisticated systems. But, late at night, while he is running a long backup program, he occasionally pores over community college catalogs and dreams of another life.

In many ways George's obsession with computers could be described as a dysfunctional addiction which kept him from normal relationships with his friends and his family. But if he had displayed the same intense interest in football or chess, his parents would have been more understanding. The school might have provided him with a coach. He might have made the team and competed with other schools, won championships, and trophies. Most of all, he would have fit into a normal pattern of life expected of him.

Computers and the Internet, like other communication media, provide both opportunities for creative expression and, when misused, attractive traps that isolate people and retard intellectual and social growth. More than anything else, George's parents and teachers needed to spend time with him while he was online. They needed to find out what made computers so attractive to him and use that carrot to guide him and challenge him to more well-rounded activities. For example, his interest in fantasy could have led him to program his own fantasy games or write stories that could have been published online. He needed the adults in his life to understand and value what he could do. This would have led to more self-esteem and perhaps to a greater ability and desire to try things outside of his computer world.

Students like George should be actively recruited by school and community computer labs, but instead of just letting them hang out and fool around, they should be taught to become integral parts of the program: helping newcomers, documenting applications, and even teaching classes. Schools, especially, should integrate computers into every discipline, to broaden their attractiveness and usefulness.

One would not provide gifted young tennis players with wooden racquets these days because it would handicap the development of proper skills and lessen their ability to compete. In the same way, every student should have the opportunity to work with the latest hardware and software. Being stuck with seriously outdated systems means that students cannot keep abreast of new ideas and trends. Because of the cost of keeping up with new technology, this should be a school and community responsibility, not just a parental one.

Students should be able to improve their computer skills as long as they have the desire to. K-12 schools should form partnerships with two- and four-year colleges to insure that advanced students can pursue their interests in formal ways without having to rely on the underground hacker world alone.

There are many places already on the Internet that support the contributions of young people. Global Show-n-Tell (http://emma. manymedia.com:80/show-n-tell/) is a virtual exhibition that lets children show off their favorite projects, possessions, accomplishments, and collections to other kids (and adults) around the world. The exhibition consists of children's artwork in the form of multimedia pages.

The Internet has the potential to harness youngsters' creative energies. They can be contributors to the worldwide information pool, not merely consumers. With more and more schools hosting their own servers, the cost of publishing a child's work online is becoming minimal. The latest versions of several word processing programs are available with HTML output as a standard option, thus making it even easier for amateurs to create Web pages with a very small learning curve. Teachers need to create opportunities for the best of their students' work to be shared. Perhaps the local poetry magazine becomes a regional electronic publication. The debating club or chess club could schedule some of its matches online. The extra time that it would take to do this could be reduced, if students did most of their work on computers to begin with and if all were routinely trained in Web publishing skills, just as grammar and composition are routinely taught today.

Perhaps the first step is to get teachers excited about the possibilities. The Exploratorium Center for Teaching and Learning in San Francisco has been holding summer institutes for K-12 teachers for over a decade. An important part of the curriculum is to have librarians experienced in electronic research work with teachers on their individual projects. It doesn't matter if the project is connected to classroom content or not because the real agenda is to get teachers excited about the project-based and inquiry-based learning. The hope is that they will go back to their schools and demand these resources for their students.

This year, during an introductory workshop on the Internet, one teacher had a conceptual breakthrough at the center. He had been politely listening to the lecture and working the hands-on exercises until he discovered the Grateful Dead home page (http:// www.uccs.edu/~ddodd/gdhome.html). His excitement knew no bounds. He went through all the text, pictures, and sounds until he discovered the lyrics section. There he noticed that a few of the lyrics were annotated but not the lyrics to his favorite songs. His first reaction was the same as if he had come upon a book that did not contain what it advertised. "Why aren't they all annotated?" he complained to the instructor. She told him that the pages were probably created by volunteer fans and that most likely no one had yet had the time to do his favorites. "Why don't you contact them and see if you can sign up to do them?" she suggested. He was flabbergasted and awestruck. It had never occurred to him that he could be a contributor. If it never occurs to the teacher, it is less likely that the student will get the idea.

An effort funded by the National Science Foundation is encouraging high school students to form project teams with students from other schools, teachers, and other adults. Through the use of advanced technologies, the Learning Through Collaborative Visualization (CoVis) Project at ·Northwestern University (http://www.covis.nwu.edu/) is attempting to transform science learning to better resemble the authentic practice of science. Traditionally, K-12 science education has consisted of the teaching of well-established facts, with the teacher taking on the role of the expert. This approach bears little or no resemblance to the question-centered, collaborative practice of real scientists.

Participating students study atmospheric and environmental sciences through inquiry-based activities. Using state-of-the-art scientific visualization software, students have access to the same research tools and data used by leading-edge scientists in the field. Students and teachers in many different schools use the Internet to work together on projects. They are assisted by scientists from universities and museums who mentor their projects and provide contextual information.

Plugged In is an important non-profit community computer center in East Palo Alto, California. East Palo Alto has been described as "an island of poverty in a sea of middle- to-high-income suburbia." Part of Plugged In's (http://www.pluggedin.org/) ambitious mission is to creatively use computers and communications technologies to support community-building efforts. Teenagers and their families are exposed to different cultural, artistic and intellectual practices. Emphasis is placed on developing models to interact across disciplines and cultures. Projects created by students are published on the Internet.

Students have spoken at several leading industry and community events. Such programs meet a vital need as we move toward an information-based society, where the ability to communicate and collaborate in new ways will be a major factor in professional and social mobility.

Plugged In's staff consists of young people who not only work on their own creative projects but who provide contract support services to businesses who want a Web presence (http://pebbles.pluggedin.org/pie/piehome.html).

In the future, children's access to the Internet will be as automatic as their access to television is today. Unlike television, it will be interactive. They will be able to participate in decisions governing their own lives. The art of writing will no longer always be just focused on the ideas of a single individual, but also be able to reflect a group consensus when that is appropriate. In time the traditional separation between the two parts of the creative process will become blurred, with the nominal author sometimes becoming the recorder of the group spirit. Barriers of age, race, class, and ethnicity will fade. Contributions will be judged on their own merits. On the Internet, no one will know if you are a child or an adult.

SCENARIO TWO: THE DREAM DEFERRED

It was a weekday afternoon in the late 1950s in a small-town suburb of New York City. Anna, a not-so-little girl, was reading the story of Pecos Bill to the school garden club. The club had been forced to stay indoors that day because of the rain. Everyone was having a good time. The rest of the club liked Anna and looked up to her, not the least because she was a fourth-grader and they were only in the first and second grades. If she felt uncomfortable fraternizing with who her peers referred to as "babies," and trying to grow a garden in a mostly concrete environment, she gave no sign of it. She was used to being different. She was tall and shy and everyone, including herself, considered her a little bit odd. She didn't jump rope or play dress-up and her Barbie doll was still in its box.

Because her family moved a lot, this was her fifth elementary school, her first in a non-rural setting. Out of a strong instinct for survival, she had evolved successful ways of coping with new situations. First and foremost, she was an observer. She used her quiet energy to pay attention to everything that was around her. She was also a wanderer, who spent many happy hours outdoors with her dog, discovering new neighborhoods, talking to trees and flowers in other people's gardens, and collecting her "treasures"—bits of broken toys, pretty rocks, and discarded items she would find in vacant lots. She was not gregarious, but chose people she could trust, places she felt safe in, activities that were interesting, but not too challenging. If she had ever stayed in one place long enough, she probably would have become more daring, because she had an adventurous spirit.

She was also an avid reader. In the past, the small libraries that rural schools had were not enough to satisfy her craving for books. This new school and this new city had two things she had not experienced before: a large school library and a very fine public library. She took to them both immediately, hanging out in the school library until it closed for the afternoon, and then staying in the children's room of the public library until she had to go home.

Her parents, who were not educated, were puzzled and a little upset by her behavior. They wanted the best for her, and were happy that her grades were good. Maybe, they told her, she would graduate from high school, something that was rare in the family, and even go on to college, a grand goal that they could hardly even imagine. But this haunting of libraries, this always having her nose in a book, this not playing with the other children was frightening to her parents. Her mother saw her as a future Clara Barton, her father saw her as the next Annette Funicello. She didn't particularly see herself as anything yet, although the school librarian was beginning to ask her to do small tasks and she found she enjoyed that work.

One day in the public library, Anna strayed from her favorite section, the 398.2s, folk and fairy tales, and found herself in the 568s, dinosaurs. It wasn't a very big section because, in the fifties, dinosaurs were not yet a media event. There were only a few books on the shelf and she chose one: All About Strange Beasts From the Past, *by Roy Chapman Andrews (Random House, 1956). Perhaps she thought it was a fairy tale collection. The first chapter was called "The Tragedy of the Tar Pits," the story of how a saber-tooth tiger got caught in La Brea. The next, "Reading the Fossil Record," told how the author explored the Gobi Desert for dinosaur bones. The words and images had a riveting effect on her. Everything she had ever wanted to read about and imagine was there: monsters, adventure, mystery. Unlike teaching and nursing, which her parents wanted her to do, this was something that fed her dreams.*

She soon finished the few books available to her in the children's room. The school library had nothing. There was no one she could share this new excitement with but she tried. Her parents were baffled. Her friends were amused. She told her teacher, who said she could do a book report on it, but only one. She was determined to learn more.

She asked if she could use the adult collection in the public library but was refused.

Eventually, inevitably, Anna's excitement ebbed. The books, read and reread and memorized, were returned to the library shelves. It never really occurred to her that the adventures she read about were real and that there was a career open to her that would allow her to enter that world. She grew older, found other interests, finished college and graduate school, becoming, to no one's surprise, including her own, a happy, competent librarian.

How can the Internet stimulate a similar nine-year- old child's curiosity today? How could the Internet have expanded Anna's world even farther?

First, the Internet offers a great deal of information about dinosaurs. Russ Jacobson, who works with the Educational Extension program at the Illinois State Geological Survey, has created "Dino Russ's Lair, The Earthnet Info Server" (http://128.174.172.76:/isgsroot/dinos/dinos_home.html) to share information on dinosaurs and vertebrate paleontology. From this server you can connect to the Museum of Paleontology at the University of California at Berkeley (http://ucmp1.berkeley.edu/exhibittext/dinosaur.html, see Figure 3), a HyperCard reference stack on dinosaurs (http://152.30.18.100/Documentation/Dinosaurs.hqx), and an online dinosaur exhibit at Chicago's Field Museum of Natural History (http://www.bvis.uic.edu/museum/Dna_To_Dinosaurs.html). Anna also could have discovered, with the Internet, that the world-famous American Museum of Natural History in Manhattan was only an hour away on a commuter train.

Second, Anna would have found an abundance of information about the field of paleontology. The Web pages of the Royal Tyrrell Museum of Paleontology in Alberta, Canada (http://www.tyrrell.com/) publish information on their field work, opportunities for the public to work on digs with museum staff. Although Anna would be too young (minimum age eighteen), the pages provide a less romantic but more accurate overview of what happens on a field expedition. Anna could see herself perhaps doing this sort of fieldwork.

The Museum of the Rockies Paleo Field Program has day-long field sessions for families with children as young as ten years old. Although it was possible that Anna could have convinced her family to visit various dinosaur sites on their vacations, it was unlikely, given their lack of understanding about her interests. She might have hooked up with a program that was closer to home.

With a computer connected to the Internet, Anna could have sub-scribed to the Dinosaur LISTSERV (listproc@lepomis.psych. upenn.edu). While it is clear to anyone lurking on the list that it is not a forum for beginners, Anna could have found many topics of interest to her. For example, there have been discussions about the links between dinosaurs and birds, the extinction of dinosaurs, a special exhibition in Hawaii, and whether Noah should have taken dinosaur eggs on the Ark instead of full-grown beasts.

Anna would have found the toll-free number of the Dinosaur Society (1-800-DINODON) and phoned for a membership packet. The packet includes a sample issue of the *Dino Times (All the News that's Old)*, a newsletter expressly aimed at turning a "child's love of dinosaurs . . . [into] a vibrant interest in science that will last a life-time."

The Internet of the future could provide Anna with opportunities to do online projects that could be published electronically. Perhaps she would be able to hook up with the adult LISTSERV and have them help her host her own list for beginners interested in the field. The Internet will surely be a place to locate volunteer activities for youth. Anna would be able to find universities with strong paleontology programs and learn what kinds of studies and abilities lead to success.

CONCLUSION

Both these stories provide a starting place for imagining the potential of the Internet to change the way we learn, and, ultimately, the way we live. There are several important points to remember in approaching a vision of the Internet to come.

The Internet is not a digitized reference book, and it is not a free phone call to an expert. It may contain resources that in the past were only to be found in libraries and universities, but at heart it is a collection of ordinary people searching for answers to their everyday questions.

A driving passion to learn the latest technology appears to be a basic instinct of young people. That's how the human species advanced from the rock to the spear. We should understand it, nourish it, and guide it so that it does not mutate into a thwarted, self-destructive passion.

The questioning process itself is the basis for the development of new Internet resources. It is crucial that users of the Internet see themselves as potential publishers of information, broadening the mix of facts, opinions, and insights.

The roles of teachers and librarians are evolving from inculcators and deliverers of canned instruction and knowledge to learning facilitators, weaving a tapestry of support to their students. Depending on the need, educators can become mentors, consultants, co-investigators, publishers, and researchers. The line between teacher and student is fading. As adults begin to see themselves as lifelong learners, they will also begin to realize the importance of their students' view of the world.

The Internet has the potential to open doors to information as infinite as the universe. However, it is more important than ever to know how to separate the wheat from the chaff and to communicate what one knows and what one wishes to find out. These characteristics create the most intriguing benefits of the Internet: to bring people together with common interests and to create a community of learning.

ABOUT THE AUTHOR

Rosemarie E. Falanga, M.L.S., is Director of Library and Information Resources at the Exploratorium, a hands-on museum of art, science, and human perception in San Francisco. She combines
traditional library science training with a strong background in computer technology, interpersonal counseling, education, and organiza-
tional development. She was a pioneer in library and information
technology in the 1980s, enabling many special libraries to enter the
electronic age. Now the 1990s, she is at the forefront of investigating
the future direction of the information profession. Her address:
Exploratorium, 3601 Lyon Street, San Francisco, CA 94123, voice:
(415) 353-0421, fax: (415) 561-0307, e-mail: rosef@exploratorium.edu

School Instructional Information Managers: Leading the Way Today to Tomorrow

Nina Little
Supervisor of Library and Instructional Information
Services
Omaha Public Schools
Omaha, Nebraska

Overview—The Numbers	
Name of School, District or State:	Omaha Public School District Omaha, NE
Number of teachers:	3,000
Number of students:	44,000
Grades covered:	K-12
Amount of money in grant or special expenditure (if applicable): n/a	

ABSTRACT

Being prepared to take advantage of information and opportunities is always important but preparedness can be especially critical when dealing in computers and telecommunications. The Omaha Public School District realizes the importance of this technological preparedness and depends on its information managers to play a crucial role in preparing schools for the Internet. The acquisition of telecommunications links, the development of a technology plan, and training have helped the district, with its information managers, take advantage of the Internet.

BACKGROUND

Pursuit of Internet access was a challenge in a large setting on the scale of the Omaha School District. The District is urban and serves approximately 43,500 students. There are seven high schools, six alternative schools, a Career Center, ten middle schools and fifty-six elementary schools in the district. Eighty buildings and 3,000 teachers can be found in this District. There is one full-time certified Library Media Specialist, called a school Information Manager, in each high school and middle school. Eighty-two Information Managers altogether serve the District.

In fifty-two of the elementary schools there is one full-time certified or "resident" Information Manager. Because of large enrollments in fifteen elementary schools, there is a "support" Information Manager to assist the "resident" Information Manager. Presently, elementary Information Managers teach scheduled classes and work with every student in the Information Center at least once a week. As you can imagine, the Information Managers are extremely busy and their time is severely limited. I supervise all of the District's Information Managers and work with a certified Information Manager on District level problems during the school year.

TERMINOLOGY

There are two terms in the District used to refer to the facilities housing information and resources in the schools. The older term is Library Media Center and the newer term is School Instructional Information Center. As you might suspect, there are two titles for the certified person in charge of the facility. The older term is Library Media Specialist and the newer term is Information Manager. The use of Information Manager and School Instructional Information Center were used starting with the beginning of the 1994-95 school year.

The change in title was an important step in a campaign to convince our audience to re-think the role of the school "librarian" or "library media specialist." We found that the perception of the school librarian to be a simple one: a person reading stories to children, checking out books, and hunting down students for overdue materials and fines. We found that the effort over the past two decades to change the image of the school "librarian" by using the name "library media specialist" has not been entirely successful.

I will never forget my first meeting with the District's library media specialists when I became their supervisor twelve years ago. One of the more experienced members of the group stepped right up to me and, toe to toe, nose to nose, let me know that she was a "librarian," not a "library media specialist!" Interestingly, in less than two years, this "Information Manager" helped me convince her parent-teacher organization, her administration, and her staff that they should use a library automation system so that her students could more easily access information.

Computers organize, access, and retrieve information. Librarians or library media specialists, like computers, sift through vast amounts of information. Librarians manage much more information than mere machines, in print, non-print, and computerized forms. Librarians help teach students and staff locate, evaluate, and apply information. We found that the best term that best illustrates the talents and educational background of this person is not librarian or media specialist but Information Manager. Indeed, where does the student go to access information? To the Information Center, and to its Manager.

LAYING THE FOUNDATION

What are the basic technological needs of a school? Electricity? Telephones? Training? Equipment? Long before the Internet, I realized that all of our school media centers should have telephones. Basically, Information Managers would be able to gather information, not in their collections, by simply picking up the phone. Long before the acquisition of personal computers in media centers, there was an additional campaign to work on the need for more electricity and properly configured outlets as well.

I constantly share information with individual Information Managers at regular meetings. Early in the technological history of the District, when we were trying to bring telephones into schools, these meetings encouraged collaborative projects between students at different schools, to justify the need for technology such as telephone lines. Any project that could remotely be related to Information Centers and involved computers, telephone lines, and modems, was encouraged. Thanks to a new understanding of the role of Information Centers, ultimately five elementary schools were equipped with telephone lines and modems. Once in place, these foundations meant that real technological progress could be sought elsewhere in the District and in the schools.

NEBRASKA'S EDUCATIONAL NETWORK

Toward the end of 1991, a pilot project was planned with the University of Nebraska at Lincoln (UNL) and the Nebraska Department of Education (NDE) Technology Center. This project would provide a link to the Internet for Nebraska school educators. In 1992, two "800" telephone lines were installed at the NDE Technology Center to make it easier and less costly for educators to access the Internet. All Information Managers in Omaha were encouraged to register and use the service, even though many did not have computers, telephone lines, and modems in their Centers. Some had access to a computer with a modem in a school lab, some had equipment at home, and some had computers with modems in college or university classes. In addition, these Managers registered administrators and staff members in their schools to this service. Needless to say, this pilot Internet project was overwhelmed in less than a year.

In response, the state government passed legislation requiring each Nebraska Educational Service Unit (ESU) to provide school districts with a hub to the Internet. The Omaha Public School District is one of two districts in Nebraska large enough to be its own ESU. As a single-district ESU, coordination of Internet efforts was easier than for those Units serving several districts. The Omaha hub was operational on April 1, 1994.

DEVELOPING A DISTRICT TECHNOLOGY PLAN

Planning was crucial to the entire technological process in Omaha's schools. This planning process paralleled the growth in Internet access by Nebraska schools. In December 1992, the Assistant Superintendent of Instruction and Special Education requested the development of a district-wide technology plan. With a short time frame, the Coordinator of Media and Technology for the District and I formulated a skeleton and rationale for the plan. The hub of technology in each school would be the Information Center.

The plan was crucial as Nebraska and its Legislature pushed technology and the Internet ambitiously across the state. We presented to the Omaha Board of Education a 28 million dollar, four-year Technology Plan. It was applauded and "heartily" accepted but not funded. When state law in 1993 called for Internet access, this plan established the format for all of the District's technological efforts. To the Board of Education, specific requests for the implementation of Internet connectivity easily fell into line with the original District Technology Plan.

WAN/LAN COMMITTEE

The bureaucracy of the technology in the District demanded that Information Managers needed to be assertive and even aggressive in the pursuit of their own technological goals on a local level. As an example, the District had formed a Local Area Network (LAN) Committee with the task of developing a LAN in the District office. The Committee, made up of representatives from General Administration, Data Processing, and the Media Technology Center, did not include any Information Managers. It was crucial that Information Managers would play a role in future decision-making bodies in the District.

In November, 1992, an Internet Committee was formed to create the ground work for the implementation of District access to Internet. Thanks to my involvement in the District Technology Plan, I made sure that I was a member of this Committee. By the end of October, 1993, The Committee developed a "Proposal for Initial Internet Access" for the Board of Education. By March 1994, the Internet Committee and LAN Committee merged to become the WAN/LAN Committee. As a result of the work of the Committees, District Internet accounts were being made available to those staff who completed seven hours of training. Information Managers played a crucial role right in the beginning, by leading these Internet training sessions.

CURRICULUM DEVELOPMENT

During the Summer of 1994, a team of Information Managers, representing grades seven through twelve, received District funding to develop lesson plans that would integrate the Internet into specific subject areas. The lessons would be presented to all Information Managers for grades 7-12 in the fall of 1994 to use with their teachers.

This successful role for the Information Managers grew only with the implementation of the District Technology Plan and the application of the Internet. Without the early efforts to put telephones and additional electrical outlets in the schools before the Technology Plan and before the Internet, none of these efforts would have been remotely possible. Information Managers took on a new role with technology, demonstrating the value of an effective information system for each teacher, administrator, and student. Information Managers worked diligently to stay current with new developments with courses, workshops, literature in the field, and conferences.

CONTINUOUS TRAINING

Continuous training is part of the regime for Information Managers in the District as new methods, hardware, and software are always being implemented. In turn, Information Managers train the staff of their schools and keep them up-to-date. For example, on September 6, 1994—Curriculum Day in the District—all Information Managers participated in a half-day training session on the basics of the Internet. Each participant was expected to lead a similar session for their staff . During the Summer of 1995, fourteen hours of additional Internet training was provided for Information Managers. This training continued on Curriculum Day—September 5, 1995—and occurs throughout the school year. Information Managers are encouraged to propose and offer training on a continuous basis for their colleagues in their schools.

THE WHOLE PICTURE

Let me give you a view of technology in the District at the beginning of 1995-96 school year. Every building in the District, including the five alternative centers and the Career Center, has two direct connections to the Internet. These connections are provided by our Educational Service Unit. Information Managers attend monthly meetings held at the District office in a lab equipped with Apple Macintosh computers, a facility where all the computers are directly connected to the Internet. Information Managers are expected to share their expertise with staff members and administrators in their individual schools.

This effort is only a beginning and, in reality, it may never be finished. Technology keeps growing and changing. The education of personnel, administration, board members, and the public continues. In addition, there will always be competing priorities for dollars, time, expertise, and personnel in any school district. A component in any plan may change or disappear. I will continue to work in providing opportunities for Information Managers to learn about the Internet and to share innovative ideas about how the Internet can be used as an educational resource.

ABOUT THE AUTHOR

Dr. Nina Little has served the Omaha Public School District in Nebraska since August, 1984 as Supervisor of Library and Instructional Information Services. Dr. Little joined the district in 1973 and has served as a high school Library Media Specialist and as a Curriculum Specialist in the area of Humanities. Dr. Little earned B.S., M.S., and Ed.S. degrees from the University of Nebraska at Omaha and a Ph.D. from the University of Nebraska at Lincoln. In 1993, Dr. Little completed a Masters Degree in Library and Information Management from Emporia State University in Emporia, Kansas. Mail will reach Dr. Little at the Omaha Public Schools, 3215 Cuming Street, Omaha, NE 68131. Telephone (402) 557-2520, fax (402) 557-2509, or send e-mail to nlittle@ops.esu19.k12.ne.us

A "Newbie" Asks

Dale E. Beasley
Teacher
St. Philomena School
Des Moines, Washington

Overview—The Numbers	
Name of School, District or State:	St. Philomena School Des Moines, WA
Number of teachers:	14
Number of students:	280
Grades covered:	K-8
Amount of money in grant or special expenditure (if applicable): None	

ABSTRACT

St. Philomena was the first Catholic school in the State of Washington to create its World Wide Web page, constructed with the use of Internet resources and advice from other teachers on the Web. Crucial in this project were Internet sites providing assistance with the HyperText Markup Language (HTML), such as the "HTML Quick Reference Guide." The ability to examine HTML tagging in well-designed home pages with Web browsers was also very useful. St. Philomena's own Web page is, in turn, a catalyst for teachers new to the World Wide Web and HTML, thanks to its inclusion of utilitarian pointers to Internet resources.

INTRODUCTION

"Nice World Wide Web home page! We're planning on setting one up, too. Can you tell us how you got started?" Every teacher just getting involved in the Internet, especially the World Wide Web, seems to ask that question. Trying to reply by electronic mail is not easy, because there is no simple answer. Let me explain.

In 1994 my friend, John Keithly, was very involved with the Internet and asked if I was familiar with the World Wide Web. I had never heard of it. He had just finished creating a home page using the HyperText Markup Language (HTML). He demonstrated his work to me on his Internet server. I found travel by hypertext—clicking on a highlighted group of words and almost immediately visiting another computer anywhere in the world—something I very much wanted to be able to do. John offered to share his HTML handiwork with me. He thought that I could create a Web site for our students, introducing them to HTML, where they could create their own pages and even display their own art on the Internet. At first, I found HTML very difficult to comprehend. I thought that there was no way I could introduce HTML to my students because I didn't understand it myself.

ONLINE SUPPORT

To be blunt, my first attempt at creating a home page with HTML was abysmal. But I was persistent by continuing to improve my drafts of the school's page with sources on the Internet. The first, and most helpful, resource to me as a beginner was the HTML Quick Reference Guide (see Appendix for list of sites mentioned in this article and their Uniform Resource Locators (URLs)). With the Reference Guide, I began to understand the meanings of HTML symbols such as the brackets < >.

Next, I ran across a message from Robert Best in Potsdam, New York looking for beta testers of his HTML editor, Web Weaver. Web Weaver made HTML work much simpler by putting all of the tags in one software product. I began to experiment with Web Weaver as a means to do my HTML work.

At this time, St. Philomena had a shell account to an Internet server. This connection only supported Lynx, the text-only World Wide Web browser created at the University of Kansas. Lynx added to my confusion visiting schools on the Web. With Lynx, I frequently saw the word [IMAGE] in a school home page. I had no idea what this message meant.

A solution to this problem arrived when I visited the server for the *MidLink Magazine*, which at the time was operated from the Discovery Middle School in Orlando, Florida. It is now available from the Ligon GT Magnet Middle School in Raleigh, North Carolina. I began communicating with *MidLink Magazine*'s editor (and also a teacher), Caroline McCullen. She suggested that I upgrade my Internet connection to support Mosaic, a Web browser developed at the University of Illinois that supports both text and images. With Mosaic, we could view graphics and art that her students were creating and posting on the Internet. She invited students from St. Philomena to submit art for display in *MidLink Magazine*.

Since St. Philomena is a small Catholic school of average means, the budget lacked the dollars needed to upgrade the Internet connection to take advantage of Mosaic. I decided to look for an "investor" to back us. A parent and businessman, Jack McCann, helped by donating the necessary funds. It paid for a full year of Point-to-Point Protocol (PPP) access to our Internet provider, Halcyon, in Seattle. With the new connection, we switched to a graphical Web browser, Netscape, which just appeared on the scene.

With our improved connection, I discovered several sites that were most helpful. The first, known as the Earth Day Groceries Project, was created by Mark Ahlness, a third grade teacher at Arbor Heights Elementary School in West Seattle. Arbor Heights actually is located not too far from where I live. I contacted Mark and complimented him on his Web page. I asked how and where he learned to do it. He explained to me that Netscape has a "view" section in the menu bar. With this feature, I could examine the HTML tagging of specific pages and understand how they were put together. This advice was a tremendous help. With each change in our home page, I began to feel better about its appearance and began developing greater confidence in working with HTML (see Figure 1).

Steve Banks of the Highland Park Elementary School in Austin, Texas was also very helpful to our efforts. Steve's fourth grade class had created an Internet project called "Trees of the World." He asked if students at St. Philomena would participate by contributing information and graphics on trees in our area. Two of our students agreed, locating information on local trees and sending pictures to Steve to add to their home page. This activity excited my students about contributing to a home page.

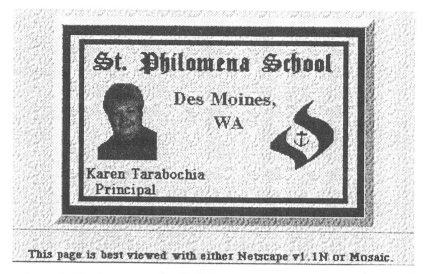

Figure 1. The home page for St. Philomena features an opening logo for the school and a digitized image of Principal Karen Tarabochia.

I decided to take advantage of this new interest in the Internet. I knew that there were excellent artists in our school. It would be neat, I thought, to have a home page dedicated to just their art work. At the time, St. Philomena did not own a color monitor. It was impossible to create any colorful graphics on the computer. The students worked around this problem by submitting work to me using traditional materials such as crayons and felt pens. I took the best of their efforts to a local copying company for scanning. At twenty dollars an hour, this alternative was expensive. I couldn't afford the luxury of working with Adobe PhotoShop and manipulating the scanned art of the students.

St. Philomena found the funds to purchase an inexpensive color monitor for the school computer. With Broderbund's KidPix, the students were able to create their own digital art. Yet with just one machine in the school, students could access the Macintosh II only during class time dedicated just to the computer, or a mere thirty minutes a week. With this sort of schedule, we began to move approximately five pictures a month to the home page. Printouts of the graphics were displayed on the Principal's bulletin board. Students were delighted to share their work with friends and parents, explaining that their work was being viewed around the world on the Internet.

The home page expanded its offerings with text as well. One teacher at St. Philomena shared a student poem and asked if it could be posted on the World Wide Web. I thought it was a great idea. From that point on, the art page for the school was devoted to both graphics and creative writing, with the text prose or poetry.

Netscape continued to improve their World Wide Web browser with additional capacity to handle HTML extensions. With each advance, the school home page continued to change. Since I wanted to have more than just information about St. Philomena on the home page, I decided to add logos to the pointers in the various parts of the school home page (see Figure 2).

I added pointers to unique science sites on St. Philomena's home page as well as pointers for anyone just beginning to learn HTML. I asked permission of those who had constructed these home pages (also known as Webweavers) if I could add pointers to their sites. I also explained that I would like to make a reduced image of logos or icons found on their pages. A listing of these sites is included in the Appendix.

I decided to promote the St. Philomena page via the Internet and assist teachers new to the Web and HTML. The school participates in two LISTSERVs designed for educators, Kidsphere (kidsphere@vms.cls.pitt.edu) and Kidlink (listserv@vm1.nodak.edu). To every teacher who introduced themselves on these LISTSERVs, I sent a message inviting them to check out our home page. To every

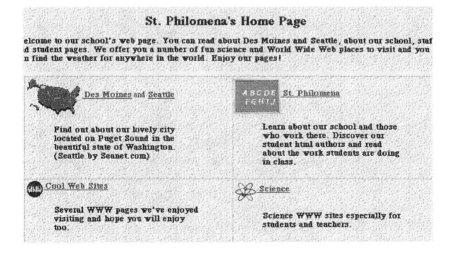

Figure 2. Logos and images from other home pages on the Web are recycled, with permission, on St. Philomena's home page.

teacher or parent mentioning that they were interested in creating a home page, I provided suggestions on how to start. Of course, my first recommendation directed them to the St. Philomena page.

In addition, I needed to get more students involved in the World Wide Web. An opportunity presented itself when the upper grades were offered a chance to participate in a six-week elective program. This program asked ten sixth, seventh, and eighth grade students to meet every Wednesday afternoon for two hours. I decided to demonstrate to this group the school home page. I explained to them that the school home page could be improved with contributions from them in the form of student pages. I explained what a student page could look like by printing for them my personal page as an example. The students enthusiastically agreed to construct a collection of custom student pages.

The first step for the students was practice with AppleWorks on Apple IIe computers in the school lab. In AppleWorks, students edited, corrected, and otherwise added to their pages to make them presentable. Once the drafts were ready, students were paired and assigned to one of the school's Macintoshes. After translating their preliminary efforts to HTML on one of the Macs, the students saved their efforts on a diskette. I helped by scanning photos of the students at a local copying center to add to their pages. In the very last session, we

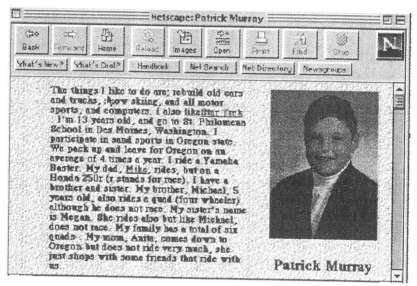

Figure 3. Individual pages for St. Philomena's students provide a brief autobiographical description and a photo.

loaded the student pages to our server and tested them. The project was a success. Now, a group of older students, experienced with HTML, will assist in the next school year with the younger HTML novices (see Figure 3).

CONCLUSION

This brief history, I hope, should help you develop your own Web site. At the age of sixty-five, I thought this new technology might be too difficult for me to learn. The old adage "You're never too old to learn" still seems to hold true. I regret that this next school year will be my last after thirty-six years of teaching. I hope to continue either as a consultant to schools interested in creating a Web presence or becoming a Web page developer myself. I envy those teachers just beginning their careers. I strongly encourage you to learn all you can about the Internet, especially the World Wide Web. It is the future!

APPENDIX

St. Philomena's home page includes the following sites. I hope you will find these helpful in creating your own home page.

HTML Quick Reference Guide
http://kufacts.cc.ukans.edu/lynx_help/HTML_quick.html
Note: A general introduction at this server to the tags, markers, and other elements of the HyperText Markup Language, it is designed with novices in mind.

MidLink Magazine: The Electronic Magazine for Kids in the Middle Grades
http://longwood.cs.ucf.edu/~MidLink
Note: This site takes pride in the fact that students are responsible for developing all their pages and graphics themselves.

Highland Park Online, Highland Park Elementary School, Austin, Texas
http://www.hipark.austin.isd.tenet.edu/home/main.html
Note: Very well developed site thanks to teacher Steve Banks, who has been promoted to Technology Director for the District.

Arbor Heights Elementary School, Seattle, Washington
http://www.halcyon.com/arborhts/arborhts.html
Note: Mark Ahlness operates, at this site, the Earth Day Groceries Project. Students decorate grocery bags with environmental themes, which are then returned to stores to be given to customers. At last count, 115 schools reported in with 45,699 decorated bags.

Arbor Heights *Cool Writers' Magazine*
http://www.halcyon.com/ahcool/home.html
Note: New site developed by teacher Gretchen Thompson at Arbor Heights Elementary for student creative writing. The page, according to its introduction, "gives students a global audience for their writing and encourages kids to publish."

ColorHex
http://www.firehorse.com/colorhex
Note: An excellent tool for home page developers that helps you select background, text, and link colors. Versions available for both Macintosh and Windows computers.

Web Weaver HTML Editor
http://www.northnet.org/best/Web.Weaver/WW.html
Note: Robert Best's excellent shareware tool for developing Web home pages. Be sure to check out both the World Wide Web Weaver and HTML Web Weaver. HTML Web Weaver was nominated for a 1995 MacUser/Ziff Davis Shareware Award.

Internet Starter Kit
http://www.mcp.com/hayden/iskm/
Note: Created by Adam C. Engst, this home page is a digital tie-in to the third edition of the "Internet Starter Kit for Macintosh" published by Hayden Books.

Global School Network
http://gsn.org/gsn/gsn.projects.html
Note: Great tool for teachers who wish to participate in projects with other schools.

Private School Resource
http://www.brigadoon.com:80/psrnet/index.html
Note: Working to set up servers especially for private schools in the Northwest.

Classroom Connect
http://www.wentworth.com/classroom/edulinks.htm
Note: A focused resource of Internet information specifically aimed at teachers and their students.

Bill Nye, the Science Guy
http://www.seanet.com/Vendors/billnye/nyelabs.html
Note: Creates excellent science films and videos on television, now available as a Web site.

Rain Forest Workshop
http://mh.osd.wednet.edu/
Note: Presented by Thurgood Marshall Junior High School in Olympia, Washington.

Franklin Museum of Virtual Science
http://sln.fi.edu/
Note: Developing excellent science projects with cooperating teachers.

NASA's StarChild Project
http://guinan.gsfc.nasa.gov/K12/Proposal.html
Note: Wonderful pictures for children of planets and galaxies taken by the Hubble Telescope.

Evaluating the Environment
http://cotf.edu/ETE/etehome.html
Note: Up-to-date reports on conditions of the environment around the world.

Volcano World
http://volcano.und.nodak.edu/vw.html
Note: Descriptions of volcanoes around the world.

Ocean Planet
http://seawifs.gsfc.nasa.gov/ocean_planet.html
Note: Smithsonian's page on the oceans, it describes sea life and the condition of the oceans.

NOAA's El Nino Page
http://www.pmel.noaa.gov/toga-tao/el-nino/home.html
Note: Explains the El Nino and its influence on weather.

ABOUT THE AUTHOR

Dale Beasley is presently employed at St. Philomena School, 1815 So. 220th, Des Moines, WA 98198, as the middle school science, math, and technology teacher. His e-mail address is dbeasley@halcyon.com and phone messages will reach him at (206) 824–4051. His home page is at http://www.halcyon.com/dale/stphil.html

Following the Internet Highway in the Sciences

Barry E. Rowe
Director of Educational Technology
Champaign Unit #4 Schools
Champaign, Illinois

Overview—The Numbers	
Name of School, District or State:	Champaign Unit #4 Schools Champaign, IL
Number of teachers:	600
Number of students:	9,400
Grades covered:	K-12
Amount of money in grant or special expenditure (if applicable): n/a	

ABSTRACT

The use of computers in the chemistry classroom parallels advances in personal computer technology, the growth of the Internet, and the development of specific Internet software tools. Champaign Centennial High School took advantage of its unique location near the campus of the University of Illinois and the headquarters of the National Center for Supercomputing Applications (NCSA) to pioneer collaboration between students and teachers with academic research in science education. Projects with the University and NCSA eventually led to development of ChemViz, a visualization program in chemistry, for students and their instructors.

A PERSONAL COMPUTING HISTORY

Do you remember the first time you saw a computer? Not the massive mainframes proudly displayed on television that filled a room, but a computer that you could actually touch, own, and even program yourself? When I started at Champaign Centennial High School in 1980, I remember fondly our first Apple II+ computers. I was a new, young chemistry and math teacher, and with a background in Fortran and BASIC, I was assigned to teach programming with these machines.

By our current standards, these computers were slow and primitive with a mere 64k of RAM, a forty-column screen, and a solitary disk drive. But at the time, these machines meant the wonderful end to input by punched cards or tape. I started to play with these computers simply by writing programs in BASIC. It was intellectually stimulating but it wasn't very practical to my classroom needs. I needed more computational ability for my classes.

When I was teaching a math course at the local community college, one of my students told me about his Sinclair ZX80 computer. It was even less powerful than the Apple II+, with two kilobytes of RAM, tape storage, and forty columns. I purchased it from him and eventually I assembled a Sinclair ZX81 with 16k of RAM, a printer, and a real keyboard, all loaded into a custom case created by a student in one of our shop classes. With this device, I was able to perform word processing, with output all in capitals. Given my handwriting, this feat was a major step forward.

From the Sinclair, I moved to an NEC 8201, a notebook computer. With forty columns, 64k of RAM, and an assembler for quick programming, it was powerful compared to my earlier computers but there was little software written for it. If I wanted a grade book program, I would have to write it myself. I also obtained a printer at the time that delivered output in both upper and lower cases. With a 300-baud modem, I signed up for CompuServe and GENIE and inflated my phone bills.

How many more computers did I use? My wife upgraded me to an Apple IIGS computer and I became enamored of the graphical interface for the first time. With this computer, I learned Pascal and worked with a wonderful group of Apple IIGS enthusiasts. Vendors such as Roger Wagner Publishing and ByteWorks were supportive, helpful, and friendly. Roger Wagner proved to be very important in my effort to use computers in education by pointing me to a program called HyperStudio (see Figure 1).

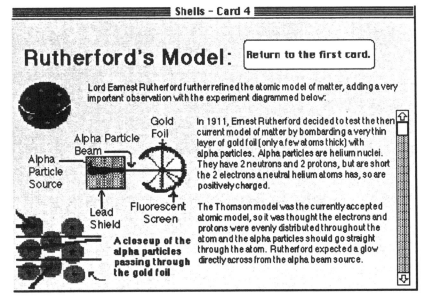

Figure 1. A view of the HyperStudio IIGS card embedded in an instructional stack on atomic theory, used in high school chemistry classes.

HyperStudio opened the world of hypermedia to me. With well-designed hypermedia programs, we could actually arrange text, sounds, animation, and graphics together in presentations for students. Students themselves could also make HyperStudio files. My personal dream of using computers to accomplish specific computational feats in the classroom was slowly becoming a reality.

One summer, I was involved in a program with two students working on science applications with computers. With the students, we manipulated HyperStudio to emulate specific experiments in chemistry. We eventually were required to present the results of our research. While other researchers had used sophisticated workstations or IBM compatible computers in their work, we found ourselves to be the only group that had used Apple IIGS computers. A University of Illinois researcher looked at our animation and remarked "Look at that slow computer. . . . Sure is a nice presentation, though. Wow, look at that animation!" I knew we were on the right track.

SUPERCOMPUTING HIGH SCHOOL SCIENCE

The initial memo looked pretty innocent. It asked for a teacher to work with a graduate student in psychology from the University of Illinois who was examining basic comprehension of science. I agreed to help, so one day Juan Moran walked into my Advanced Placement Chemistry class. Mr. Moran wanted to experiment with my best class. We tried to find ways to understand how students visualized abstract chemical concepts. We choose molecular theory and focused on shapes of molecules. We videotaped the students constructing molecules with balls and sticks and discussed the tapes with chemists and chemical educators. We realized that some of the best chemistry students didn't understand how to visualize in three dimensions and we were disappointed. We needed a method to help them visualize molecules in an easier way.

Dr. Nora Sabelli, of the National Center for Supercomputing Applications (NCSA) at the University of Illinois, contacted me about my interest in visualization. She had heard about my work from the University's chemistry department. She thought a computational method for visualizing atoms and molecules developed at NCSA could be used by high school students to make their own virtual models of atoms and molecules.

I tried the program and realized that it could not be used by high school students in its initial form. It took me a whole day to learn how to invent a model with NCSA's Cray-2 supercomputer, a well-connected Macintosh, and vi, the operating system's visual editor. I explained to Dr. Sabelli that there had to be alterations in the program to make it useful to high school students. With a National Science Foundation (NSF) grant, we improved it so that students could make their own models of atoms and molecules. This project became known as ChemViz (see Figure 2). Information on it is available at http://www.ncsa.uiuc.edu/edu/ChemViz/ (see Figure 3).

ChemViz continues today. We have trained field testers and have completed many experiments using the program with kids. Its growth has led us to other projects, even to the point of evaluating new grant proposals to NSF.

CHEMVIZ AND THE INTERNET

In the course of our work, we discovered that complex visualization files were very difficult to transfer over phone lines with modems. The Internet would have been an ideal medium but at that point our schools were not connected. The ChemViz team of chemistry teachers tackled the problems and arranged Internet connectivity for each of our schools. How? By leveraging the ChemViz project as the rea-

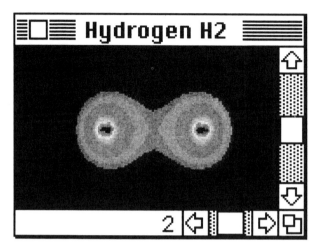

Figure 2. Champaign Centennial high school student Justin Hill created this view of a hydrogen molecule.

son for Internet in the classroom. But we wondered among ourselves if ChemViz really justified the expense of an Internet connection.

At one fortuitous ChemViz meeting, a member of the NCSA staff described a new program that would make the Internet easier to use. It was called Mosaic. Since we had Internet connections, she asked us if we would like to test Mosaic for NCSA. We agreed quickly, taking advantage of a school lab with Macintosh LC computers connected to the Internet. My ChemViz colleagues also jumped at this unique opportunity.

Mosaic in its earliest state crashed frequently but that did not deter the students. Eventually, with a stable version of the program, students were finding information all over the world on the Internet. We decided to post information about ChemViz on the Internet, using high school students to construct HyperText MarkUp Language (HTML) documents. One student, Ed Thomson, even discovered how to write forms in HTML.

NETWORKING AND EDUCATION

Following this, I interviewed and was selected as the district's Director of Educational Technology. On the first day in the new post, the Superintendent and I discussed networking. Why network? What are its advantages? He was very interested in the Internet and networking. I brought to these sessions a missing component—practical classroom use of the Internet.

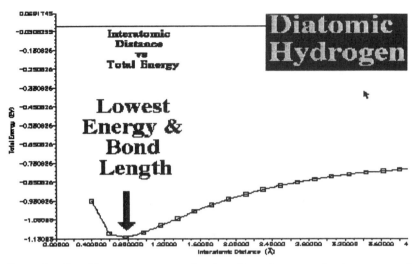

Figure 3. ChemViz can create graphs describing, for example, the energy of a molecule versus bond length.

We formed a team to enhance networking and the Internet in the schools. This effort eventually brought together a neighboring school district; Ameritech, our phone provider; and the University of Illinois. We implemented a network that connected all of the schools, classrooms, and offices to the Internet. Individually, this team included teachers, students, administrators, parents, University staff, and community members. In turn, networking and the Internet focused on student learning. We made a philosophical change from classroom-focused education to student-focused education, where individual students have more control of their education with Internet resources.

Networking has provided some real advantages. For example, with e-mail students and teachers work with experts and participate in research projects. E-mail encourages the development of pen pals and markedly improves communications. In the classroom, networks allow expensive equipment to be shared, keeping expenditures for hardware low for the entire system.

FUTURE POSSIBILITIES

We expect classes and students to continue to collaborate over the Internet. Video conferencing and video presentations over the Internet will make this sort of collaboration more realistic and timely. School resources will continue to be shared even more easily as networks improve. Networking within the school, to other local schools and institutions, and to the larger Internet community encourages new possibilities for every member of the community (see Figure 4).

ASSISTANCE

There are many places where you can find help with networking and the Internet. Universities often have a mission to help public schools so local institutions of higher education are a good place to start. There are grants available from federal agencies such as the National Science Foundation to help schools with networking as well. Private industry can be of assistance, too. Phone and cable companies occasionally have specific programs to assist schools with online strategies. Finally, look to state, regional, and local governmental agencies. Some of these agencies are ready to help schools by providing the means to create an infrastructure that will support networking.

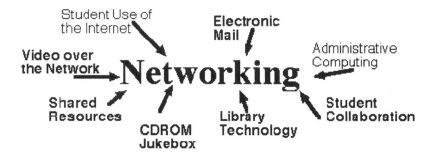

Figure 4. Networking is central to student, teacher, and staff use of technology.

ABOUT THE AUTHOR

Barry E. Rowe taught mathematics, physics, chemistry, computer science, hypermedia, and multimedia for twenty-four years in various schools in central Illinois. He is now Director of Educational Technology for the Champaign Unit #4 Schools and a consultant to the National Center for Supercomputing Applications (NCSA), in chemical visualization. He has B.S. and M.S. degrees from Illinois State University. He is currently involved in networking the Champaign and Urbana schools. His e-mail address is browe@ncsa.uiuc.edu and his address is 703 South New Street in Champaign IL 61820, phone number (217) 351–3756, fax (217) 351–3871. His major hobby is restoring TVR sports cars.

A Statewide preK-12 Model for Internet Connectivity

Wayne Fisher

Internet Specialist
Education Technology Center
Nebraska Department of Education

Overview—The Numbers	
Name of School, District or State:	Nebraska Department of Education Lincoln, NE
Number of teachers:	21,000
Number of students:	350,000
Grades covered:	K-12
Amount of money in grant or special expenditure (if applicable): $2.5M to put regional (ESU) supporting infrastructure in place	

ABSTRACT

Students can best prepare for this information and technological age through experience with the Internet's rich resources. As a consequence, all students should have equal telecommunications opportunities. Nebraska solved this problem by developing its own Education Network to provide connectivity for all preK-12 schools. But connectivity without support would have been disastrous so Educational Service Units and other programs were integrated into the process. The success of Nebraska's telecommunications efforts prove that the educational community can work harmoniously with state agencies and corporations to find solutions to large-scale and convoluted problems.

NeNET

The Nebraska Education Network (NEnet) was developed to provide connectivity for Nebraska's preK-12 educators and schools. At this point, user accounts are primarily assigned to preK-12 teachers; there is limited direct student access. With a wide array of services, teachers use the Internet to communicate and collaborate with colleagues and mentors, participate in curriculum projects, and collect resources through e-mail, newsgroups, telnet, and Gopher and World Wide Web servers.

The frequency of Internet access by teachers appears to depend on the integration of the Internet into curriculum projects. Many teachers use their accounts at least once a week to check for and send e-mail. Student use of the Internet is limited to closely supervised sessions with highly structured tasks. As security issues are resolved and acceptable use policies developed, more students will access the Internet.

There are nineteen education service agencies, called Educational Service Units (ESUs), in the state of Nebraska. They are crucial to the logistics of the Internet in the state. Nearly all of these Units or ESUs are directly connected to the Internet by T-1 lines, providing more than adequate bandwidth for their regions at the rate of one million bits per second. Each ESU acts as the Internet hub for the schools within its service area (see Figure 1).

Schools reach their Internet hub either by directly dialing into the ESU or by connecting with a 56k line (56,000 bits per second). Each Educational Service Unit across the state is connected to Lincoln and the State Department of Education (NDE). NDE in turn links to the State Division of Communications (DOC), along with other state agencies. DOC then plugs the entire state into the broader Internet pathway through a major Internet provider (see Figure 2).

HISTORY

Nebraska's Internet story tells of both key partnerships among state agencies and grassroots efforts in communities. It begins near the end of 1991, with discussions between the State Department of Education (NDE) Technology Center and the University of Nebraska at Lincoln (UNL). A pilot project was created, with the University providing Internet links for teachers. NDE was asked to simply provide an electronic mail server.

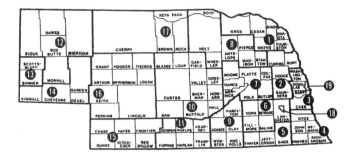

SU #1	Wakefield	@mother.esu1.k12.ne.us	ESU #10	Kearney	@genie.esu10.k12.ne.us
SU #2	Fremont	@esu2.esu2.k12.ne.us	ESU #11	Holdrege	@courier.esu9.k12.ne.us
SU #3	Millard	@esu3.esu3.k12.ne.us	ESU #12	Alliance	
SU #4	Auburn		ESU #13	Scottsbluff	
SU #5	Beatrice		ESU #14	Sidney	@panesu12.k12.ne.u
SU #6	Milford	@esu6.esu6.k12.ne.us	ESU #15	Trenton	@esu15.esu15.k12.ne.u
SU #7	Columbus	@gilligan.esu7.k12.ne.us	ESU #16	Ogallala	@esu16.esu16.k12.ne.u
SU #8	Neligh	@pluggers.esu8.k12.ne.us	ESU #17	Ainsworth	@esu17.esu17.k12.ne.u
SU #9	Hastings	@esu9.esu9.k12.ne.us	ESU #18	Lincoln	@lps.esu18.k12.ne.us
			ESU #19	Omaha	@ops.esu19.k12.ne.us

Figure 1. Nebraska Educational Service Unit (ESU) regional hubs with a listing of Internet Protocol (IP) domain name addresses.

By the middle of 1992, with the financial help of the Nebraska Math and Science Initiative (NMSI) and the technical help of the University, the NDE Technology Center purchased an Internet-connected, multi-user Sun SPARCstation workstation. Since most educators had to make a long distance call to the University to use this connection, online time was limited. Two "800" phone lines were eventually installed to minimize the long distance costs. Some fortunate educators were able to work around the long-distance charge by connecting to the NDE host computer via a nearby state college or university.

Over 2,500 Nebraska teachers asked for accounts in less than a year. The overwhelming popularity of this Internet option and the heavy demand on the "800" phone lines caused NDE to considerably overrun the budget set aside for the pilot project. In spite of the costs, the project was an excellent strategic move, in providing an introduction to the Internet for teachers, proving the need for greater bandwidth, and beginning the slow but important process of integrating the Internet into the curriculum.

During the 1992-1993 school year, several events occurred in the state capitol that improved connectivity across the state. First, the State Division of Communications (DOC) worked in tandem with the state's forty-two telephone companies to construct a network backbone, using Frame Relay technology. Frame Relay provides 56,000

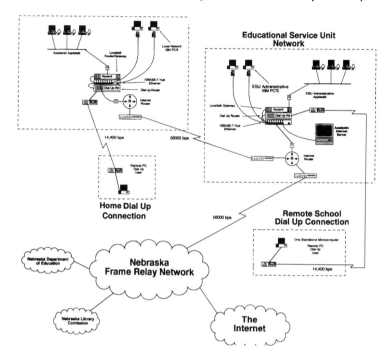

Figure 2. A schematic of Internet connectivity in Nebraska, bringing it down to the most basic level in schools and homes.

to 1,500,000 bits per second available as simply a local connection. For many rural schools, this sort of connection is very attractive and considerably reduces the costs of high-speed and reliable Internet access. Also, Frame Relay has been successfully used in other states with large rural populations, such as Utah.

At the same time, Senator Ron Withem, Chairman of the State Legislature's Education Committee, held hearings across the state to assess the needs of Nebraska educators. Thanks to the success of the Internet pilot project and general enthusiasm for the Internet, one consistent message was sent to the Education Committee from teachers: improve connectivity to the Internet.

The Education Committee and Chairman Withem heard the message. They consulted with Melodee Landis, Director of the NDE Technology Center and Jim Lewis, NMSI Program Director, in putting together new legislation to improve connectivity. A bill, LB 452, was drafted to increase the number of Internet hubs and to provide training and support. It was introduced into the State Legislature, passed, and subsequently signed by the Governor on March 4, 1993.

CONNECTIVITY

LB 452 directed the ESUs to provide a direct connection to the NDE for schools and to organize training and support to users. Tax authority was granted to fund this effort and guidelines were established for districts and schools. By April 1, 1994 the Internet "switch" was literally turned on at the ESUs. Schools were now able to directly connect with a 56k line to their ESU or dial in.

For those schools using a dial in connection, only one computer and one modem could access the Internet at a time. In some cases, long distance charges were difficult to anticipate in advance and control. Even though a 56k line was initially more difficult and expensive to set up, it enabled schools to have multiple simultaneous users at a consistent monthly fee which made the budgeting easier. Plus, this dedicated sort of connection meant that computers at home could reach the Internet directly via a local phone call to a school in the community (see Figure 3).

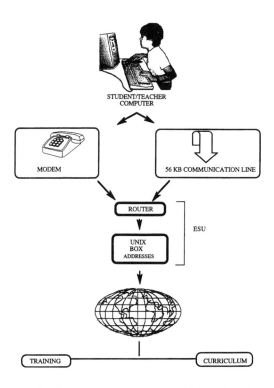

Figure 3. Options for Internet connections in Nebraska schools.

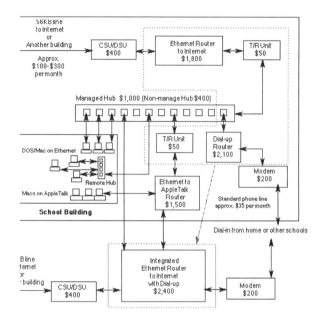

Figure 4. A scenario for the design of an Ethernet local area network (LAN) and wide area network (WAN).

Nevertheless, some of the technical hurdles were difficult for even the most motivated schools. One of the major telephone companies in the state helped by providing technical expertise. Given that successful connectivity to the Internet would increase the overall use of phone lines and ultimately generate increased revenue for the telecommunications providers, it is not surprising that there would be those companies who would assist us with acquiring, installing, and configuring 56k lines (see Figure 4).

Eventually, with a strong infrastructure in place as a result of the legislative initiative in the form of LB 452 and excellent training from staff at the ESUs, Internet use in Nebraska grew exponentially. This phenomenon fueled the demand for even better Internet connectivity. The Legislature was again petitioned to provide additional funding directly to schools, to help with local connections for schools. LB 860 was drafted, introduced, passed, and signed by the Governor in June, 1995. This law requires the direct connection of every school building in the state to the Internet by June 30, 2000. Also, every school building in the state will be wired completely for computer networks.

BENEFITS

The approach of schools in Nebraska to the Internet has produced several benefits. For users, Internet access is easy because it is consistent and straightforward. All teachers share a common suite of Internet options providing resources most appropriate and valuable to preK-12 education. Extensive Internet exploration for appropriate resources isn't necessary.

Support is also consistent and straightforward. A "train-the-trainer" strategy used across the state makes support easier and more efficient. In addition, curriculum resources and training materials are routinely reviewed to provide up-to-date and topical information quickly. This approach keeps costs down and overhead low.

Low costs were maintained by capitalizing on the distributed nature of the Internet wherever possible. For example, Internet accounts are served regionally by fifteen ESU hubs, distributing the task of support statewide to thousands and thousands of users. This approach means that smaller and less inexpensive Internet host computers can be used across the state rather than one large, expensive, and centralized mainframe. The temporary crash of any one host does not cause the entire statewide system to fail. In a centralized system, the temporary failure of a centralized mainframe indeed would bring down the entire statewide Internet service. From a maintenance perspective, this distributed approach is highly attractive.

Each ESU configures its computer and network connections in the same way. This consistency makes remote management and monitoring of the network possible across the state. Resources that require high maintenance are placed in one location, at NDE, to minimize the management load.

DESIGN

Nebraska's approach to the Internet can evolve as demand grows thanks to its flexible design and scalable architecture.

What does flexibility mean? Not all schools are able to progress at the same rate toward connectivity. Does the state's overall plan penalize late or early adopters? Different kinds of connections, by modems or dedicated lines, can be handled easily and efficiently as schools are ready to participate. Both technical support and training are designed to meet the needs of individual schools. Infrastructure does not have to be altered radically at each ESU as increasing numbers of schools link to the Internet.

With Frame Relay as the preferred statewide communication system, the costs of equipment at each ESU and for each school is low. In our plan, a school is linked to the nearest Frame Relay access point. Then, via a permanent virtual circuit or PVC, a link is made to the nearest ESU. This approach eliminates the need for large and expensive routers (costing some $30,000 to $40,000) at each ESU. Instead each hub, or ESU, needs only a $3,000 router, providing as a result considerable savings.

Thanks to the combined vision of teachers, legislators, and administrators, eventually all Nebraska schools will be connected directly to the world through the Internet. This vision will become a reality thanks to partnerships with the state's phone companies resulting in more favorable telecommunications rates and the additional beneficial use of inexpensive networking equipment. These factors have combined to place the Internet within the grasp of most districts, regardless of size and budget.

PROSPECTS

The magnitude and complexity of this sort of task can be overwhelming, whether it's connecting an entire state to the Internet or just an individual school. Take heart, others have gone before!

What does it take to move a state towards an Internet strategy? In the early stages of this sort of work, a strong individual or small groups are needed. They have to be highly committed to the project, becoming the catalysts to make everything happen.

It is extremely important to constantly evaluate the latest technologies as they develop and as you implement your plan. At key points, you must make the best decisions you can, based on the information you have at the time. Recognize that the hardware you choose now will improve in the future and cost less. As a hedge against ever changing technologies, be as adaptable and compatible in your equipment choices as possible. Implement your project with open systems. Proprietary solutions will ultimately prove to be restrictive and expensive.

There's no doubt that implementation of telecommunications technologies is complex and time consuming, whether it is applied to a single school building or across the state. The rewards are tremendous. Access to the rich resources of the Internet will provide tremendous rewards to citizens in your community, especially the youngest.

ABOUT THE AUTHOR

For six years, Wayne Fisher has been with the Nebraska Department of Education in the Technology Center, where he was originally a general Instructional Technology specialist. Over the past four years, he has specialized in the area of telecommunications and the Internet. More recently he has gained considerable expertise in the area of wide area network (WAN) connectivity and building-wide computer network wiring design and standards. Wayne is a former high school chemistry and physics teacher and has an M.S. in Education from the University of Nebraska, Lincoln. His address is NDE Technology Center, 301 Centennial Mall So., Lincoln, NE 68509, phone (402) 471–2085. His e-mail address is: wfisher@nde.state.ne.us.

Part II:

Building Models

Internet Infusion Models: Uses of the Internet in a Suburban K-12 Public School District

Donald E. Jacobsen
Technology Support Specialist
Millard Public Schools
Omaha, Nebraska

Overview—The Numbers	
Name of School, District, or State:	Millard Public Schools Nebraska
Number of teachers:	1500+
Number of students:	17,000+
Grades covered:	K-12
Amount of money in grant or special expenditure (if applicable): n/a	

ABSTRACT

Millard Public Schools is a suburban school district located near Omaha, Nebraska. With over 1500 staff members serving in excess of 17,000 students, Millard is the third largest school district in Nebraska. Every classroom in all twenty-nine schools has at least one high-speed data connection to a wide area network (thirty-one buildings total) and access to the Internet. Some 500 K-12 students have been involved in teacher-guided Internet Field Tests that use both home and school connectivity. Thanks to a growing number of staff obtaining Internet accounts, many students have been using this technology under teacher guidance. It is anticipated that, in the near future, student use of the Internet in Millard will continue to grow rapidly.

INTRODUCTION

Few would disagree that instantaneous access to information is a positive development. However, bringing information into the classroom and focusing it into the meaningful delivery of instruction can be challenging. How have teachers brought, or infused, the Internet into their classrooms? This article describes successful classroom Internet applications as well as a number of practical problems that had to be solved by teachers, on nearly a daily basis.

This paper briefly describes School Board-approved field tests of student Internet use over the past two years. Each student was directly guided by a cooperating teacher. Students applied for Internet accounts and agreed to a district-adopted, appropriate use policy for the Internet. Each student accepted this policy, which was also signed by the student's parent or guardian. Nearly 500 students were involved, some having both home and school connectivity. Only one occurrence of inappropriate use was documented in literally thousands of Internet sessions. Limited filtering of newsgroups, provided by the Nebraska Department of Education, is responsible in one way for this record. No other session management or monitoring software was used at the district level.

For the 1995-96 school year, high-speed connectivity to every classroom has been achieved. A dramatic increase in Internet use should occur with the completion of the network and site-based curriculum infusion projects. Further details can be found at http://esu3.esu3.k12.ne.us/districts/millard/mps/

SECONDARY AND MIDDLE SCHOOL INTERNET PROJECTS

The Millard South High Meridian Club Project was awarded a Peter Kiewit Foundation Teacher Achievement Award in 1994. In this project, high school Physics students measured the circumference of the Earth using the length of shadows cast by fence poles at a tennis court. Since this experiment required two measurements from different locations on the same meridian (96 degrees west longitude), information was collected and passed rapidly between participants by e-mail. Mr. Steve Skinner was in charge of this project which involved about 125 Physics students who collaborated primarily with counterparts in Broken Arrow, Oklahoma and elsewhere along our meridian. The project proved to students, teachers, and parents that the Internet could provide real time exchange of scientific data, in this case involving the location and angle of the sun. The goal was to accurately measure the circumference of the earth and even challenge accepted figures. The outcome has been very consistent and repeatedly confirmed semester after semester. This project involved history and mathematics teachers in an interdisciplinary effort to make cultural as well as scientific exchanges along the meridian from Canada to Mexico. Participants in the project were recruited through a science newsgroup on the Internet.

Local, state, and national awards for a unique application of tech-

Figure I. Senior High School students and their instructor work on the Meridian Club Project, sending e-mail to Oklahoma with data on the circumference of the earth.

nology in the classroom have been achieved by a project called Physics Online at Millard North High School. Originally funded in part by a grant from U. S. West, this project provided physics students with an opportunity to use telecommunications resources both in school and at home. Students accessed a database of physics problems and review materials on the Internet. They also received interactive assistance with homework, using e-mail to find help from sources such as the Massachusetts Institute of Technology's Advanced Math and Physics Help Desk. Students additionally accessed the Internet and published on the World Wide Web, with a computer secured with a Toyota Tapestry Grant.

The Red Planet Project was an interactive and multi-disciplinary endeavor to complete an imaginary mission to Mars. Participating high school students were drawn from math and science classes. The Internet was used to access information at NASA, science and engineering laboratories, and many university libraries. Students also collaborated with NASA researchers and engineers who were working on space travel projects. The Internet was the vehicle to discuss, develop, and approve (or disapprove) of acceptable mission scenarios. The Internet expanded the time frame available for the project since ideas were not limited to those that could be devised in just a fifty minute class period. The medium of the Internet also equalized discussions so that dominant students in class had less impact on the outcome. More introverted students made greater contributions to the group.

The French Connection allows students to correspond with "sister" French classes in Europe, Canada, and the South Pacific. This endeavor at Millard South High School was facilitated by Mrs. Kathy Hardenbergh and Mrs. Kay Knyffeler and involved about 40 different students. The objective was to promote written communication and cultural exchange with students in France and Canada. Students read and react to news, contribute to online projects, and use the chat formats of the Internet to discuss global issues, all in French. In addition, the students used this project to develop plans and itineraries for their summer trip to France, made reservations for hotels and transportation, and determined which restaurants they would visit, all via the Internet (see Figure 2). As with all these projects, the outcomes are overwhelmingly favorable as students declare increased involvement and engagement in the learning activities. Quantitatively, these students have shown an increase in test scores on the national exams that is significant.

Persuasive Writing on the 'Net has given Advanced Placement English students the ability to work with a university English composition class. By exchanging papers over the Internet, high school students worked with college students, and their professor, in editing and rewriting sessions. This interaction meant that the high school students' papers have been more thoroughly researched. In addition, writing techniques have been reinforced by involving a third party—college students—in the learning process. (see Figure 3)

Advanced Placement and Challenge German students have used the Internet to access information written in German, from German sites, for presentations for class. Students developed their presentations with Internet-based resources and presentation programs such

Figure 2. High school students chat in French over the Internet during the French Connection Project.

as Hyperstudio, Aldus Persuasion, and Microsoft PowerPoint. In class, students exchanged insights based on their study of German Internet resources and facilitated classroom discussions of German literature and current events. Students are also developing a QuickTime video for a tour of their school in German. This video will be compressed and published on the Internet via the district World Wide Web home page.

Finally, the first Middle School home page was developed by students with the assistance of media specialists, studying HTML or the HyperText Markup Language in a course on computer applications. Graphics, audio, video, and numerous links to school and classroom information were used. The home page contains nearly two hundred links, with information on city and state history, school calendars, local and world weather, class and curriculum projects, and student information.

ELEMENTARY SCHOOL INTERNET PROJECTS

One of the most interesting uses of the Internet at the elementary level has been a project in which students at the Norris Elementary

Figure 3. Students use e-mail during a peer editing session in their Persuasive Writing class.

School developed their own home page. With the home page, students provided general information about their school and information about the school's namesake, George W. Norris, a famous Nebraskan. Each grade level and subject area, such as music, physical education, and media, have links on the home page pointing to other sites. Graphics and audio were also incorporated in the form of student-created art and even a floor plan of the building (see Figure 4) was included.

Some of the strategies involved in this effort included cooperative learning, research and writing skills, computer applications, and multi-age group and interdisciplinary learning. Students found this project fun and informative, and the project itself moved at a very fast pace. Students have been motivated by the success of it to continue to update and administer the home page.

In another effort, the Millard Education Foundation awarded a grant to two elementary schools to teach twelve students and their parents about the Internet. The children, and at least one of their parents, attended a two-hour session once a week for seven weeks to learn how to use e-mail and World Wide Web browsers. Students and parents worked collaboratively on presenting multimedia reports to their

Figure 4. Elementary students construct their World Wide Web home page for their school.

classmates on the resources they found on the Internet (see Figure 5). Skills related to reading, writing, grammar, research, and technology were all involved in this project. Students also saw first-hand how adults could be life-long learners.

The project called "Are There Legos on the Moon?" was perhaps the most creative of the elementary technology projects. Developed and guided by Mr. Denny Hanley of Sandoz Elementary, this project had sixth graders using the Internet to converse with engineering students at the college level for problem solving techniques related to maneuvering a Lego machine on a moonscape. Students, for example, used information gathered on the Internet to create an accurate replica of a portion of the Moon. They then assembled a motorized Lego robot and controlled it with a personal computer to travel over their reconstructed Moonscape and perform certain kinds of tasks. E-mail and files downloaded from museums and research projects contributed to this project. The Moonscape itself was visible to robot controllers only via a videotape feed. This feed was recorded and transmitted over the Internet with "CUSeeMe" for real-time interaction with other, remote participants (See Figure 6).

About 25 students were involved in this effort and the outcomes

Figure 5. An elementary student discusses his World Wide Web research with his class.

achieved were once again qualitative. "Best thing we ever did" . . . "A fun way to learn" . . . "A different approach to school" . . . were among the exit interview comments from the kids.

DISTRICT PERSPECTIVE ON THE INTERNET

The future of the Internet in the Millard Public Schools is very exciting. Our experiments with the Internet have encouraged the District to formulate large and integrated Internet plans. For example, with the Millard District home page, we will provide access to information and resources specifically designed for Millard educators and staff. It will also provide a structured starting point for exploring the Internet via the World Wide Web. The Millard Director of Public Relations will contribute a segment on District events as well as general information for patrons and the public. District administrators will put together information on major issues, such as curriculum, personnel, and strategic planning. Information related to staff development and registration for professional classes will be accomplished online.

We also plan that Millard's Technology Support Services will post current versions of freeware or District site-licensed software on a

Figure 6. Elementary students browse the World Wide Web for information to assist in their "Legos on the Moon" Project.

server, so staff can access programs with File Transfer Protocol (FTP). In addition, all documentation and training materials will be available electronically. Pointers to Web sites related to the curriculum, organized by grade level and subject matter, will also be accessible.

Each school and administrative building in the District will post information on the home page through local administrators. Not only will information become immediately accessible to users, but we assume that the District will reduce dramatically a great deal of paperwork previously generated by memos and handouts. We anticipate considerable cost savings and less waste as a result.

CONCLUSION

Millard Public Schools recognizes the significance of telecommunications technology and the Internet for students entering the work force in the next century. We have tried to position ourselves to prepare our students for this future. In spite of unpredictable changes in this technology, especially in hardware and software, we are committed to meeting the challenge of preparing our students and striving for excellence.

ABOUT THE AUTHOR

At the time he wrote this article, Donald E. Jacobsen, PhD. was a Technology Support Specialist in the Millard Public Schools. He has undergraduate and graduate degrees in biology along with fifteen years of secondary classroom teaching experience. He is currently involved in Information Management Services at the H.P Smith Ford Motor Company. His mailing address is 5051 L Street, Omaha, NE 68117 and he can be reached by phone at (402) 733–8100 or fax at (402) 731–7959. His Internet address is djacobso@novia.net.

Internet Access and Curricular Use in Wisconsin Schools

Neah J. Lohr
Consultant
Microcomputer and Instructional Technology
Wisconsin Department of Public Instruction
Madison, Wisconsin

Overview—The Numbers	
Name of School, District or State:	Wisconsin Department of Public Instruction Madison, WI
Number of teachers:	66,812
Number of students:	860,686
Grades covered:	K-12
Amount of money in grant or special expenditure (if applicable): n/a	

ABSTRACT

Statewide efforts in Wisconsin since 1990 have concentrated on providing electronic connectivity for all 426 school districts or some 2,000 individual schools. Especially significant in the past few years have been plans initiated by the State Legislature, such as the Wisconsin Telecommunications Act (1993 Act 496). These programs to encourage the use of technology in schools continue in the 1995-97 Wisconsin biennial budget.

INTRODUCTION

Dial up? Terminal emulation? Direct connect? SLIP or PPP? Commercial vendor? WISCNet? BadgerDial? These terms and phrases carry enormous implications for many educators in Wisconsin wrestling with Internet realities for their schools. Faced with an increasing need for Internet connectivity, more Internet options, and declining budgets, these options have become very important to school board members, administrators, teachers, and community members.

Wisconsin currently has 426 school districts with slightly over 2,000 school buildings located in rural, suburban, and urban areas. Districts, governed locally, range in size from under 300 students to over 95,000 students in preK through grade twelve classes. Twelve regional Cooperative Education Service Agencies (CESA) work with all of the schools in the state. These CESAs offer a variety of services, depending upon the needs of the schools.

HISTORY AND BACKGROUND

Over the past several years, there have been several attempts to connect school districts, public libraries, CESAs, state and local government agencies, and colleges and universities to assist communication, collaboration, and access to digital resources. These efforts have encouraged new projects aimed at improving connectivity to electronic information and sharing scarce resources.

What does the situation look like in general in Wisconsin? In a 1994 survey, only 8 per cent of small and rural community (under a population of 10,000) schools had Internet access. Some 32 per cent of medium size (10,000-49,999) community schools were connected to the Internet. Fifty-nine per cent of schools in communities of over 50,000 were linked to the Internet.

WiseNet (*Wisconsin Education Net*work) is one solution to improving access to basic kinds of educational information for state schools. Developed and maintained by the Wisconsin Department of Public Instruction (DPI), WiseNet transmits educational information around the clock to any location in Wisconsin via a toll free number. The WiseNet bulletin board system provides school districts and CESAs quick and easy access to information from around the state and nation, bypassing the traditional system of printing and mailing. The system features electronic mail, educational news section, a special interest group board, and file transfer capabilities. WiseNet has been a good place for educators to start communicating electronically, however, it does not offer an interface to the Internet so it will be phased out as other Internet-functional systems (such as BadgerDial) become operational.

Another fast and free online service for Wisconsin educators is called Learning Link Wisconsin, provided by the Wisconsin Education Communications Board. It features forums and e-mail and is also accessible at any time. Educators use it to explore curriculum development, enhance classroom lessons, and discover professional development opportunities. One unique feature of this service, Curriculum Connection, coordinates instructional television programming with curriculum development and classroom lessons. It also offers users a connection to the Internet for e-mail; expanded Internet options are planned. Due to demand on Link's toll free number, users are limited to fifteen minutes per connection with a maximum of sixty minutes of online time per day.

WISCNet

In Spring 1991, the higher education data network known as WISCNet became operational. It was originally comprised of all twenty-six institutions in the University of Wisconsin System and eight private colleges and universities in Wisconsin. WISCNet was formed and partially funded over a three-year period through National Science Foundation (NSF) support in the form of a $589,000 grant. This network provides high-speed 56k (56,000 bits per second) and T-1 (1,500,000 bits per second) lines to connect to other networks such as CICNet (a network of all of the Big Ten universities plus other selected institutions) and NSFnet as well as national computational resources. It also provides communication among researchers and teachers with access to the Internet.

Since WISCNet was only partially funded by the NSF grant, initial startup costs for each member were $12,000 for a node and $14,500 annually for maintenance at each site. Those costs for members have since been reduced considerably. The Madison Academic Computing Center (MACC) on the University of Wisconsin (UW)-Madison campus was originally hired to provide maintenance and keep the network in operation. The Department of Information Technology (DoIT) at UW-Madison currently maintains the network.

The high costs of access to WISCNet were prohibitive for the state's school districts. The Wisconsin Department of Public Instruction realized the increasing importance of electronic communications so efforts were made to fund a connection between schools and this higher education network. Proposals emphasized staff development, especially enhancing the expertise of science and math teachers. Unfortunately, these suggestions were not funded.

Some institutions of higher education have been cooperative individually in allowing school districts near their campuses to take advantage of campus connections. The costs for these back-door, dial-up arrangements have ranged from nothing to up to $2,000 per year. With the increased use by schools of these sorts of connections and their demand for more bandwidth and support from their higher education colleagues, there have been changes in the relationships between schools and universities. For example, some schools that once paid no fees for connectivity now incur minimal charges. Nevertheless, for many schools, this option is nearly impossible since the nearest college connection is an expensive long-distance phone call away.

VISION

A plan was needed for schools throughout the state to gain access to electronic resources beyond a piecemeal approach. DPI's Division for Libraries and Community Learning approached the problem by developing an "Internet Access Policy Statement and Plan" which has been subsequently adopted. The Plan, in summary, calls for every educational and library organization in Wisconsin will have full and dedicated (not dial-up) access to the Internet by the year 2000. In addition, by the year 2000, every Wisconsin resident will have dial-up access to the Internet through a toll-free telephone call.

Meeting these will achieve five important objectives. First, use of the Internet will be promoted and facilitated by schools and libraries to carry out their missions. Second, the Internet will be used to share information among all types of libraries. Third, the Internet will provide information to education and library communities as well as the public, from state agencies such as the Department of Public Instruction (DPI). Fourth, the Internet will be utilized by employees of DPI and all other state agencies. Finally, the Internet will be used to carry out programs and services of state departments and divisions.

Specifically, this Plan will be carried out by the DPI's Internet Work Groups, in coordination and cooperation with state agencies as well as education and library communities in Wisconsin.

STATUS

To further this Plan, several efforts are currently in progress. Through the use of an Ameritech grant, all state agencies now have newly installed direct connections to the Internet. The Department of Administration (DOA) has recently established a state Gopher called "Badger," or the Wisconsin State Agency Internet Gopher (gopher://badger.state.wi.us). The Department of Public Instruction (DPI) has been working with DOA by contributing information to the Gopher server. Electronic links from the DPI menu have been made to other Gopher servers created by the U. S. Department of Education, other state education agencies, the Library of Congress, and the American Library Association. The Wisconsin Department of Public Instruction also has its own home page, containing numerous files and over 200 links to other sites (http://www.state.wi.us/agencies/dpi).

BADGERDIAL

In May, 1995, the Department of Administration's (DOA) x.25 "lottery line" became available to educators for statewide access to the Internet using a Serial Line Internet Protocol (SLIP) connection. This program is called "BadgerDial" and represents a cooperative effort between Ameritech, the Department of Administration, the Department of Public Instruction, and the Department of Information Technology on the UW-Madison campus. It will provide a basic level of Internet access throughout the state at a reasonable cost. The start up cost is fifty dollars including a complete software package with applications such as Netscape. For a ten dollar monthly fee, users receive ongoing twenty-four hour, everyday support. Line charges from any location in the state are eight cents per minute. DPI's Division for Libraries and Community Learning staff will be involved in training school and public library users in the use of this connection. BadgerDial is one attempt to address the issue of equity of access to electronic information in the state.

A proposal to the U. S. Department of Commerce to upgrade BadgerDial was recently approved, providing $250,000; the Wisconsin Department of Administration is providing an additional $500,000 for the effort. The project will provide online access to WISCAT (Wisconsin Union Catalog, the largest bibliographic database in the United States); upgrade and strengthen connections to BadgerDial throughout the state; subsidize the connections of low income school districts for a year; and provide training on the use of the Internet. DPI staff will be heavily involved in the implementation of the project while the regional CESAs will focus on development, training, and ongoing support.

Wisconsin also received a planning grant to develop connectivity models for ten counties in the state. With this grant, there will be an effort to create tools that are both user-friendly and disabled accessible. Another part of this grant will help develop an improved state and local infrastructure action plan, setting priorities and timetables with funding recommendations. It will be developed by project engineering consultants and interagency teams.

WISCONSIN TELECOMMUNICATIONS ACT (1993 ACT 496)

On July 5, 1994, Governor Tommy Thompson signed "1993 Wisconsin Act 496" deregulating the state's telecommunications industry. Effective September 1, 1994, the Act implemented some of the recommendations of the Governor's 1993 Blue Ribbon Telecommunications Infrastructure Task Force. The legislation established a new regulatory model for telecommunications utilities, reflecting a more competitive marketplace.

Thanks to this law, the Wisconsin Public Service Commission (PSC) regulates utilities with the goal of developing alternative forms of regulation, promoting competition, infrastructure deployment, economic development, consumer choice, and universal service. The law provided an immediate 10 per cent rate reduction for Ameritech residential and small business lines. Local residential service, standard business, and small business usage rates are frozen for three years. Annual price increases may be deferred for a maximum of three years into a single increase, but limited to 10 per cent or the increase in the gross domestic product price index, whichever is greater.

A Universal Service Fund will be established to ensure affordable service to low-income customers as well as rural and other areas of the state. Starting on January 1, 1996, telecommunications providers must contribute to this Fund in proportion to their gross operating revenues from intrastate telecommunications services. Many consumer protections are also included in the law. An Advanced Telecommunications Foundation was established to support technology projects and educate consumers about advanced services. Priority will be given to projects in school districts where the expenditures per student are below state average spending levels. This includes a "Fast Start" provision of $5,000,000 targeted for technical applications in the schools. The foundation will have a fund of over $40,000,000, with the state contributing $500,000 and the balance from private industry.

As a direct result of this legislative action, Ameritech, one of the telecommunications providers in the state, made a commitment to bring fiber to all of the high, junior high, and middle schools in its territory. It will also provide a 'just in time' service for elementary schools that are ready to use fiber. Ameritech will invest at least $700 million in new equipment and technology during the next five years, expanding fiber connections to include colleges, universities, vocational schools, and major public libraries.

Another provider, the General Telephone Company, indicated that they will grant $2,500 to each public and private school in their territory to offset costs of technology projects and enhanced services. In addition, GTE will grant $1,500 to each public library in its territory to assist in the use of new technologies. These grants will be in the form of billing credits over the next four years to meet yet to be determined criteria. Ameritech and GTE represent the largest of the state's nearly 100 telephone providers and they serve the largest population.

WISCONSIN'S BIENNIAL BUDGET

These developments have encouraged state initiatives in technology. In the most recent biennial budget for 1995-97, several provisions are aimed at providing funding for educational technology to schools. These opportunities could be used for Internet connectivity. For example, the "Pioneering Partners" program establishes a nine member Educational Technology Board (ETB) to administer some $10,000,000 in grants for educational technology and distance learning. Another $15,000,000 in trust fund loans will be available for implementing, expanding or participating in projects approved by the ETB.

CONCLUSION

Changes in telecommunications regulations, diverse connectivity plans, and structured programs will assist Wisconsin in taking advantage of Internet resources. Diverse options provide numerous opportunities ultimately to lower costs and enhance connections for all of

Wisconsin's schools and libraries. With additional state funds and grants from federal agencies and corporations, Wisconsin will be one of the leaders in the use of the Internet for education and information retrieval.

APPENDIX

Selected home pages of a few Wisconsin schools

Belleville School District
http://joe.uwex.edu/~k12/Belleville/index.html

Kaukauna Electra Quinney Middle School
http://athenet.net/~joker/

Madison Middle School 2000
http://198.150.8.9/

School District of Marshfield
http://www.uscyber.com/education/marshfield-k12/

Washington High School, part of the Milwaukee Public Schools
gopher://whscdp.whs.edu:70/1

ABOUT THE AUTHOR

Neah J. Lohr has classroom teaching experience in grades K-8, taught computer literacy for grades 3-12, and was a library media specialist and district media director in a K-12 school district. She is now the microcomputer and instructional technology consultant at the Wisconsin Department of Public Instruction. She is also the team leader of the Instructional Media and Technology Team in the Division for Libraries and Community Learning at the department. She is a frequent speaker on automating library media centers and integrating computer technology into classroom curriculum. Lohr has a masters in library science and completed the specialist program in educational administration, at UW-Madison. Neah J. Lohr can be reached at the Wisconsin Department of Public Instruction, 125 S. Webster Street, P. O. Box 7841, Madison, WI 53707-7841. Phone (608) 266–3856 or fax (608) 267–1052 with e-mail to lohrnj@mail.state.wi.us or to lohrnj@macc.wisc.edu

Education on the Info Highway: the Nueva School, NuevaNet, and PIPE

Ray Olszewski
Computer Systems Specialist
The Nueva School
Hillsborough, California

Overview—The Numbers	
Name of School, District or State:	The Nueva School Hillsborough, CA
Number of teachers:	25
Number of students:	320
Grades covered:	pre-K–8
Amount of money in grant or special expenditure (if applicable): n/a	

ABSTRACT

Nueva School, a private pre-K-8 school in California, established itself as a premier educational user of the Internet over the course of twenty-four months. In the summer of 1993, the Nueva School was assigned an Internet domain. It was the first elementary school in California to operate its own domain on its own equipment. Connectivity was assisted by teachers, alumni, and friends, with costs borne by the school itself, grants, and donations. These efforts delivered substantial dividends as the school and its faculty became significant members of the collaborative effort known as the Peninsula Internet Partners in Education (PIPE).

INTRODUCTION

At the Nueva School, we believe strongly that children acquire skills most effectively in authentic contexts. These contexts allow kids to learn and practice skills in projects that they find meaningful. Computer-related skills are an important part of this process. Yet, skill in using the Internet is not immediately valuable to a typical ten-year old. We needed to develop a program of Internet training that would teach long-lasting skills to be a valuable foundation for our students well into the future. And we needed to teach these skills through applications of the Internet in our existing curriculum in mathematics, writing, the humanities, science, art, and music.

At first, the process of doing this Internet work was far from clear. But we knew that we had to try something or it would never become understandable on its own. So several of us—the school librarian, the computer specialist, several homeroom teachers, a few parents, alumni, students, and I—started to work on the Internet.

AT THE BEGINNING

As we started, we thought we were well equipped to take advantage of the Internet. The school's computer lab featured sixteen new Apple Macintoshes; respectable, we thought, for a school with 320 students. Computers in most classrooms supplemented the lab, giving a means for kids to continue on projects between sessions in the actual lab. In addition, almost all of the students' homes were equipped with computers. Fortunately, we had just wired the elementary school building with both Ethernet and Apple LocalTalk network connections. LocalTalk linked the middle school to the elementary school network hub. These links gave students access to hardware and software, especially those in grades three through six, where the computer program was the strongest.

Alas, cabling and networking were more costly than we had expected or allowed for. Nothing was left in reserve for a server. Rather than abandon our plans, we utilized a rebuilt and under-powered 486 computer operating Linux. Linux is an implementation of UNIX for IBM PC-compatibles that, at that time, was just starting to become popular in some circles.

The server worked, most of the time. The decentralized community of highly collaborative Linux developers was releasing new kernels almost weekly. The server itself had too little memory and hard disk space (see Figure 1). But it gave the staff the chance to move online, to explore new possibilities, and to improve their Internet skills. Over the next few months, our online abilities improved quickly. (See Figure 1)

For staff, we organized workshops and informal sessions that introduced many to the basic Internet services of the time: e-mail, File Transfer Protocol (FTP), Gopher, and Usenet newsgroups. Back in 1993, the use of World Wide Web browsers was just beginning. In retrospect, it is clear that we under-invested in training and staff education. For example, we were unable to schedule Internet training during in-service times. As a result, only staff with sufficient interest to learn, on their own time, took part in the workshops. One-on-one tutoring was tremendously effective but like all such tutoring, it was an expensive use of trainers' time.

All but our youngest Nueva students take regular computer classes. In these classes, older students were introduced to some of the Internet tools that could be accessed directly from their Macintoshes. Gopher, for example, was a quick hit. Many students quickly took advantage of research and recreational resources found with Veronica searches as well as with pointers to Gopher servers. Admittedly, these

Figure 1. NuevaNet in the "old days" of 1993 when our physical facilities had a spit-and-bailing-wire look. We worked hard to make NuevaNet appear a bit more professional.

research activities were not always entirely curriculum-based. For example, sixth-grade boys seemed to suffer from a fixation with Cindy Crawford. On a routine basis, we searched and trashed an impressive variety of images that exposed Crawford to varying degrees.

Still, in this early stage, only a few staff and students developed real expertise in the use of basic Internet services and tools such as e-mail and Gopher. Those demonstrating Internet talent were not always the best computer students or the most technically sophisticated staff members. Motivation seemed to be more important than prior experience with new computer resources, in finding useful information that provided the impetus for additional practice and exploration. Even the fascination with Cindy Crawford was not all to the bad. After that obsession, we never had to explain Gopher or Veronica to any of the older boys!

The Internet was, and still seems to be, fairly demanding for those depending on Web and Gopher servers. Patience is tested when, for example, entire sites disappear overnight. The most hardy computer users suffer when connections are refused with only the most cryptic explanations. Indexing can be fragmentary and out-of-date. Networks and tools occasionally exhibit an unreliability that is common perhaps only at the cutting edge. The Internet indeed requires self-motivation.

For the staff, the school librarian and I searched for resources in the sciences, humanities, and writing. We encouraged our colleagues in the school to subscribe to LISTSERVs mailing lists and to visit routinely education-related Gopher sites. This intense search enhanced my own expertise in locating Internet resources and in using Internet tools. These experiences combined two specialties—traditional library research skills and the odd mix of mental flexibility and rigidity that's a basis for a knack for technology. The range of resources on the Internet and their sometimes now-you-see-it-now-you-don't nature amplified the problems of evaluating the quality of information.

Our expertise, though acquired quickly, led us to several opportunities, most notably the beginning of what would become the PIPE Consortium.

PIPE

The Peninsula Internet Partners in Education, or PIPE, is a group of public schools, a museum, and a private school (Nueva) collaborating on the development and delivery of curricula via computer networking. In the summer and fall of 1993, we organized the first collection of PIPE schools and solicited support from foundations. We succeeded in a big way with three supporters.

Pacific Bell's California Research and Education Network (CalREN) Foundation chose PIPE for a pilot project in the use of ISDN for computer networking, a service capable of carrying 128,000 bits per second. With CalREN's support, we set up an extended LAN that linked Nueva with our initial group of eight public schools. These schools all used our domain for school-to-school communication and collaboration, as well as access to the Internet.

The Peninsula Community Foundation gave PIPE seed money to support training, and also allowed staff to participate in collaborative projects. These funds also provided technical support for the evolving consortium and the extended LAN. Hewlett-Packard helped PIPE with an equipment grant that included hubs, a new server, and other networking equipment.

UPGRADING HARDWARE AND SOFTWARE, INCREASING ACCESS

While we were working on creating the proposals that led to those grants, we were forced to deal with a server that just was not very reliable for our growing number of users. Fortunately, by early 1994, Linux itself had matured into a reliable and reasonably stable operating system. But our hardware was increasingly undependable. Fortunately, a small infusion of funds permitted the purchase of a new and improved Linux-based server. It arrived in February, 1994 and allowed us to add accounts with confidence. It sported sixteen serial ports, giving us the means to install a bank of eight modems to provide dial-in access to NuevaNet.

The next few months saw a big spurt of activity as we expanded our selection of Internet services and tools. Volunteers worked with me to install a Gopher server, a Web server, an automated system to manage discussion groups, and more. Students and parents in large numbers signed up to NuevaNet, increasing the number of accounts from thirty to over 600. Internet access was being used both for schoolwork and for personal enjoyment. Although the curriculum still did not integrate the Internet formally, more ambitious students and staff individually discovered many new resources. Nueva staff and PIPE members worked on developing a new Internet-based curriculum, and looked for ways to incorporate the Internet into the existing curriculum.

A few curriculum-based projects were developed. For example, our seventh graders worked on "Country Report," in which each student completed in-depth research on a foreign country. Results by the class traditionally were presented at a "Country Night" to staff and parents. As an established project, it demanded that students use many resources to learn about their assigned countries. Internet resources expanded research options. The Internet allowed students to directly contact citizens in different countries with e-mail. It also gave students access to both official and other kinds of information via Gopher and Web servers as well as tidbits on LISTSERVs and Usenet newsgroups.

In this geographic research, the sometimes disorganized state of Internet resources provided some unplanned bonuses for students. For example, one girl developed a passionate interest in the rights of

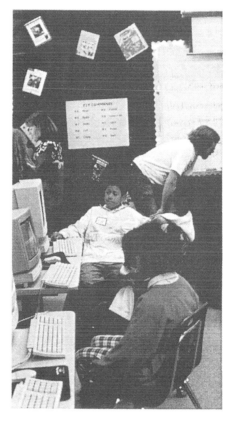

Figure 2. Although the Peninsula Internet Partners in Education emphasize electronic collaboration, from time to time participants still need to meet in person. In this case, students from Nueva and Chavez Academy work at Nueva on the final version of the PIPE collaborative newspaper.

women in India through information she found on a Usenet news-group and a LISTSERV. The class as a whole learned about the geography of the Internet, particularly how little Internet connectivity exists to eastern Europe and sub-Saharan Africa.

The most successful of our early curriculum projects was called the "Forties" project, in which third and fourth grade classes studied the events of the decade of the 1940s. Access to the Internet enriched this project in many ways. Especially valuable was ElderNet, a LISTSERV of older men and women many of whom were children or adults during World War II. Students corresponded with a man who lived in Scotland during the War; a Canadian who fought during in the War; several women who left their homes to work in the War effort; and others.

With PIPE funding, we began intensive training for teachers and librarians. Training included sessions on the use of Internet resources and tools as well as an explanation of how these resources could be used in the curriculum and in collaborative projects. This training effort continues to show its value. Those staff who have participated are both the most knowledgeable about and the most committed to using the Internet in education.

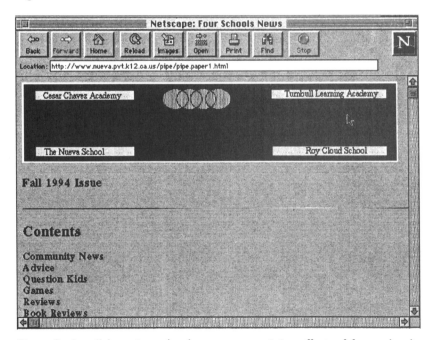

Figure 3. A collaborative school newspaper, a joint effort of four schools, appeared in both paper and digital forms.

NEW VENTURES

The 1994-95 school year began with teachers at Nueva and among our PIPE partners ready to try several curriculum experiments. With equipment from Hewlett-Packard (HP), I spent much of the fall preparing for, then converting to, a high-capacity, RISC-based HP server. This server supported the addition of more Internet accounts and greater access for all. It also provided the bandwidth to support new curriculum-based projects. Over the summer, I installed and tested ISDN bridges that allowed PIPE partners to share a single, extended LAN to communicate among themselves and to access the Internet.

Point-to-Point Protocol (PPP) capability was also added to our dial-up lines, giving NuevaNet users the ability to establish a direct (but temporary) connection to the Internet, instead of one mediated through an Internet host. With PPP, our users began to work with a full range of Internet applications at home, including World Wide Web browsers; Fetch, an FTP client; TurboGopher, a Gopher client for the Macintosh; and Eudora, an e-mail assistant. Available first to Macintosh users and later to Microsoft Windows users, PPP increased the ways in which students could reach NuevaNet from home. It also encouraged parents to become involved in computer activities with their children.

There were several successful projects for the school year. With "Mudfellows," students collected samples of mud from the periphery of San Francisco Bay. They dissected the mud, identified its contents, and prepared a report entitled "Field Guide to the Mudflats of San Francisco Bay." The guide was published in paper and electronic forms. It can be found at http://www.nueva.pvt.k12.ca.us/pipe/pipe.mudguide.html

"Footprints" was a math project designed for sixth graders. Kindergarten and first-grade students tabulated personal data about themselves, such as sex, birth date, hair and eye color, and foot size. This information was shipped over the Internet to a sixth-grade class at Nueva. Students used ClarisWorks to analyze the information and produce presentations for the younger students. The final results were published as a multimedia presentation called "Looking at Children" created with the program, MacroMedia Director.

"Community Newspaper" was a collaborative newspaper prepared by four partner schools. Students at each site were responsible for organizing and editing a portion of the newspaper (see Figure 2). Students used e-mail to solicit and collect material. The final product was

Figure 4. NuevaNet provides a complete online tour of the campus, with information about individual teachers and programs. In this example, information about the Library is available to students, teachers, parents, and other interested parties.

prepared in both print and Web editions (see Figure 3). It is posted at http://www.nueva.pvt.k12.ca.us/pipe/pipe.newspaper.html

"Infobrokers" enabled all of the PIPE librarians to share their resources. This project also trained older students in library skills by requiring them to answer research questions posed by younger students (see Figure 4).

FUTURE CHALLENGES

1995-96 marks the third year of the Nueva and PIPE experiment with the Internet in elementary education. We have achieved a lot, but we continue to face challenges. Computer technology, networks, and the Internet are changing rapidly, and we need to keep up. For Nueva, that means improving our hardware. We are in the process of upgrading some portions of our LAN and looking at ways to extend the Ethernet to the middle school. The middle school currently is limited by a slower LocalTalk network.

In addition, we need to develop our presence on the World Wide Web. Although Web growth has been explosive, much of it has been commercial. We think that the portion of the Web dedicated to elementary schools has grown more slowly. We are looking for ways to add useful resources for K-8 educators on the Web.

Finally, we need to integrate the Internet more closely into the curriculum. We will improve in the areas where we have already been successful, such as in the social sciences, the humanities, and writing. We need to increase resources dedicated to math and science. A sixth-grade course called "Applications of Computers to Mathematics" will use some Internet resources. Another program called Archinet will help students use the Internet to learn about architecture and collaborate on playground designs. The library will focus on using the Internet for literature searches and locating experts for assistance with science fair projects.

LESSONS TO BE LEARNED

We have learned some important lessons. First, start small—but start! We began with a good network and flaky equipment. As we learned more, we improved NuevaNet incrementally. This approach allowed us to develop our expertise so that we could acquire equipment and outside services intelligently. Our hard-won experience and judgment let us distinguish our real needs from what others wanted merely to sell to us.

Second, use volunteers but use them carefully. NuevaNet owes its existence to parent and alumni donating time, expertise, and considerable funds. Most schools have similar resources in their parent and alumni communities. But as you work with volunteers, remember that their experience with computers and networks is usually outside a school environment. We had to educate our advisors about the realities of limited school budgets. For example, casual suggestions that we solve a problem with a commercial software package required quick calculations and even quicker explanations: "software that costs the school $300 per client times thirty computers in the school equals $9,000. That's more than our annual budget for upgrades." Decisions about server security had to reflect our need to keep access so simple that even a child can do it.

Third, anticipate change and realize that your are not working with bricks and mortar. Three-year-old computers are almost antiques and six-year-old ones work well as boat anchors. In the last two years, the Web has grown into the service most associated with the Internet in the minds of new users. Many older computers simply cannot deal with demands of the Web. For example, some Web-based software requires nothing less than a PowerPC. To benefit from Internet advances, you will need a network that can be improved incrementally. You will also need the funds to make these enhancements.

Finally, develop expertise among your staff in the use of computer networks. To be most effective, this sort of education needs to be part of the job and it needs to be rewarded. Whether you encourage participation through training, or with free or heavily subsidized computers for teachers in their homes, or simply with time set aside in the course of a day for practice, you will need to support the growth of Internet expertise among your colleagues.

ABOUT THE AUTHOR

Ray Olszewski is Computer Systems Specialist at the Nueva School, a private pre-K-8 school in Hillsborough, California. He is responsible for managing the NuevaNet LAN and Internet domain; teaching a sixth-grade course known as Applications of Computers to Mathematics; and coaching the Nueva Science Fiction Writing Workshop. He also teaches workshops on the Internet, networking and the

World Wide Web. Ray also provides instruction in computer programming in BASIC and C. He also acts as a consultant to schools and other organizations.

Ray can be reached by e-mail to ray@nueva.pvt.k12.ca.us or to ray@comarre.com or via the Web at http://www.nueva.pvt.k12.ca.us/~ray/ Fax messages may reach Ray by dialing (415) 344–9302 (Nueva) or (415) 322–1209 (consulting office). Mail can be sent to the Nueva School at 6565 Skyline Boulevard, Hillsborough, California 94010 or to the consulting office at 762 Garland Drive, Palo Alto, California 94303. The URL for the Nueva School is http://www.nueva.pvt.k12. ca.us/ With considerable difficulty, Ray can be contacted by voice at (415) 348–2272 in the Nueva School or at his consulting office at (415) 321–3561.

Boulder Valley Internet Projects

John R. Speckien
Project Coordinator
Creating Connections
Boulder Valley School District
Boulder, Colorado

Overview—The Numbers	
Name of School, District or State:	Boulder Valley School District Boulder, CO
Number of teachers:	1,882
Number of students:	26,000
Grades covered:	K-12
Amount of money in grant or special expenditure (if applicable): n/a	

ABSTRACT

The Boulder Valley School District is located thirty miles northwest of Denver, Colorado, covering 580 square miles and includes nine communities. Four of the nine are small, isolated mountain communities. There are altogether forty-seven schools in the District, with several new schools under construction. The District serves some 26,000 students and includes nearly 1900 faculty. The Boulder Valley Internet Project involved two major efforts. The first effort connected a large school district to the Internet with training for students and staff. The second project, called Science and Math Initiatives, continues to support math and science education in rural communities with the Internet.

BOULDER VALLEY INTERNET PROJECT

The Boulder Valley Internet Project (BVIP) began in the summer of 1991 under the direction of Project Director, Libby Black. Primary funding was provided by the National Science Foundation (NSF) and the Boulder Valley School District. Initially, six schools—one elementary, three middle, and two high schools—were connected to a District host by either high-speed ISDN or T-1 lines, moving information at rates up to 1,500,000 bits per second. The remaining schools in the District accessed the Internet over phone lines with modems.

Twenty-one teachers were given release time, support, and training to learn about the Internet and evaluate how it might be used in the curriculum. This group became the core training group for the District, training an additional eighty staff. At present, there are twenty-two training classes for staff and administrators, free and with District in-service credit. The classes range from an introduction to the Internet to specific techniques on integrating the Internet into certain disciplines.

Ultimately, several teachers in each school will act as Internet experts. Each school will decide on how to make its local expert available. Several schools are studying released time or involving student assistance. The District's management is site-based, leaving many decisions in the hands of individual schools.

CONNECTIVITY

All teachers and students are offered an Internet account with full access that can be utilized both at school and at home. At present, there are no time restraints on usage, but there is a storage limit. Several hundred students and over 200 teachers are active users of the Internet in the District. The number of users will jump dramatically with the installation of T-1 lines in every school. The District modem pool includes thirty-two 28.8 kilobits per second modems with Point to Point Protocol (PPP) software. With PPP, students and teachers can use graphical Internet interfaces from home with the right equipment and software.

A contract, approved by the District legal staff, is issued to anyone applying for an Internet account. Students applying for Internet access sign the contract and provide a social security number. A teacher as well as a parent or guardian co-sign this contract. For staff, the contract only requires the staff member's signature and social security number. At present, members of the community are not eligible unless they are directly involved with District committees or volunteer to work in the District. The contract is available at http://www.c3.lanl.gov/~jspeck/SAMI-home.html

We have had minimal problems with student use of the Internet. A complete procedure has been created to deal with violations of the contract's terms and it is possible for a student to lose permanently Internet access. Only one part of the District is not available to students, the Instructional Resources Center (IRC). Access to the IRC is only possible with a parent or guardian. In addition, Internet connectivity is provided to graduating seniors until October 31 after their graduation. This time frame gives them the opportunity to locate Internet service through a private provider or as a student in a college or university.

A group of students provides online help and support for everyone in the District. Students in these positions are trained and provided with their own support. This component has saved time and funds for the District. A complete Internet training manual is available in every school media center and it is updated constantly. The manual contains most of the material from training sessions, which have been well tested. These materials save time for individual schools in inventing their own programs.

A document entitled "Factors for Success in K-12 Networking: Observations from the Boulder Valley Internet Project" was prepared in the autumn of 1994. It addresses planning and policies; technology and its management; training and support; learning and the curriculum; and current issues. This document can save a district a tremendous amount of time and effort. A copy can be obtained by contacting Libby Black at connect@bvsd.k12.co.us

CREATING CONNECTIONS

The second major project in the District is called "Creating Connections: Rural Teachers and the Internet." Sponsored by the District and funded by Annenberg CPB/Math and Science Project, the U. S. West Foundation, the National Science Foundation, and other organizations, it attempts to meet three basic needs for rural education. First, it connects rural teachers to Internet training with twenty regional training sites. Second, it provides technical and curriculum support for participants for two years. Third, it gives rural teachers an easy-to-use and Internet-accessible database on math and science reform initiatives and data. These goals have expanded as the project has been implemented.

The first goal of the project was completed in the summer of 1994. Twenty training sites in scattered geographic locations, from Alaska to South Carolina, were chosen. These sites were all donated by post-secondary institutions, such as teachers' colleges or departments of education in universities. Many sites supported participants with free Internet accounts, technical support, and ongoing workshops.

Twenty-six participants were chosen to begin an intensive two-and-a-half-day workshop at each site. Lodging, meals, travel support, a stipend, training materials, and two years' worth of support were provided. Some twenty-one sites were actually involved.

The second goal is ongoing with support provided in several ways. Online, participants use e-mail to reach the project coordinators. Off-line, an "800" phone number is available along with fax access. A newsletter is also published and sent to each participant. Participants are asked to try two projects in their classrooms using the Internet in math and science instruction. Projects are documented and included in the project's database for further reference.

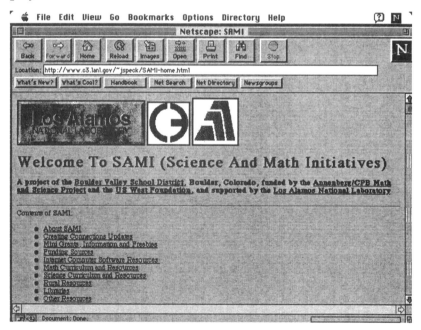

Figure 1. The home page for the Science and Math Initiatives (SAMI) project is housed at the Los Alamos National Laboratory and supported by ongoing work on the project itself.

The four mountain schools in the District are working on curriculum applications of the Internet in math and science. Their efforts are supported by two project coordinators. Online courses will also be offered on implementing national standards in the math curriculum. These courses will explain the standards and show examples of problems connected to the standards. Participants will also learn how to use alternative assignment techniques.

SCIENCE AND MATH INITIATIVES

The third goal is also ongoing. The Science and Math Initiatives (SAMI) database has grown into a one-stop shopping center for participants and has become a popular Web site. Housed at the Los Alamos National Laboratory, it is available to anyone at http://www.c3.lanl.gov/~jspeck/SAMI-home.html. It is also possible to reach SAMI by telnet and Gopher (see Figure 1).

SAMI is updated on a daily basis during the school year. It contains information on mini-grants, details on free computer equipment, software resources, and links to other sites. In addition, staff and participants are creating a resource called SAMISM or SAMI-Solve-Me. It will provide challenges to students and teachers at all grade levels and assist in the implementation of national math standards. SAMI now contains hundreds of links to educational sites around the world. Requests are received daily to add new sites to SAMI. These are evaluated and if a site is deemed beneficial, it is added.

CONCLUSION

We had originally expected that telecommunications would simply be a new avenue for rural schools to explore. We imagined that these schools would connect to other schools of similar size and interests. Although these scenarios have occurred, we also discovered that communications within specific schools has improved thanks to participation in these projects. With something new and dynamic, it is no wonder that staff were ready to share their experiences with their colleagues.

APPENDIX

For further information on these projects, contact:

Libby Black
Project Director
Boulder Valley Internet Project
Boulder Valley School District
P. O. Box 9011
Boulder, CO 80301
phone: (303) 447-5090
e-mail: connect@bvsd.k12.co.us

John R. Speckien
Project Coordinator
Creating Connections
Boulder Valley School District
P. O. Box 9011
Boulder, CO 80301
phone: (303) 447-5092
e-mail: speckien@bvsd.k12.co.us

Randy Sachter
Project Coordinator
Creating Connections
Boulder Valley School District
P. O. Box 9011
Boulder, CO 80301
phone: (303) 447-5092
e-mail: rsachter@bvsd.k12.co.us

ABOUT THE AUTHOR

John R. Speckien is the project coordinator for Creating Connections and has taught high school mathematics, chemistry, physics, and computer science. He was the technology coordinator for the Boulder Valley School District for ten years and the Senior Technology Consultant for the Colorado Department of Education. He has consulted on educational technology throughout the United States and elsewhere. He can be reached at the District, P. O. Box 9011, Boulder, CO 80301 or by phone at (303) 447–5092, fax (303) 447–4254, e-mail: speckien@bvsd.k12.co.us

Telecomputing in Smart Schools

Charles Stallard
Hampton City Schools
Hampton, Virginia

Overview—The Numbers	
Name of School, District or State:	Hampton City Schools Hampton, VA
Number of teachers:	1,750
Number of students:	23,463
Grades covered:	K-12
Amount of money in grant or special expenditure (if applicable): n/a	

ABSTRACT

Although the Internet, networking, and telecomputing have become hot topics in today's educational circles, educators should approach these with caution and a studied approach. The Hampton City Schools' Smart Schools technology program defines how to successfully integrate telecomputing into the educational process. In our plan, telecomputing is organized around reengineered school library media programs which have been renamed Centers for Information Services. Information Center specialists have become the primary supporters for the entire information infrastructure in our schools. Working with teachers and students, we continue to grow our Smart Schools through new pilot programs and projects.

INTRODUCTION

Telecomputing has been a viable part of the learning infrastructure for Hampton City Schools since 1990, when the district first initiated its Smart School program and began building local and wide area networks. Access to the Internet has been a part of that infrastructure from the beginning. Internet services for our schools continue to evolve and expand as our local infrastructure matures and as the nature of the Internet itself changes. To understand our approaches to the Internet, you must first consider the paradigm that drives all of our technology programs.

In brief, Smart Schools are completely "networked," which means that they are connected to one another and to a variety of outside resources. Staff in these schools use the networks, connections, and information to better adapt school programs to individual learners. Staff also use the empowering qualities of technology to be more productive. We are finding that telecomputing also accelerates a personalized approach to the curriculum. We think there is a logical progression in how we implement this vision. Essentially, we build the infrastructure first and then bring resources online as they are needed.

INFRASTRUCTURE AND STAFFING

Our goal has been to link all classrooms, offices, labs, and teaching and learning areas into a district-wide network. The hub for the networked Smart School is the school library, which we have renamed the Center for Information Service. The new name better describes the type of activity, the range of resources, and the changing nature of school libraries in our District. In these Centers for Information Services, most Internet and telecomputing activity occurs under the staff supervision.

The local dimension of our information infrastructure is of primary importance. Without the networked computer in the classroom or the lab, access to information resources will be limited, regardless of the resource or its location. Once learning and work spaces have been networked, we then bring in a broad range of information resources, including the Internet. With an overall computer-to-student ratio of eight students to one computer in the District and a high school ratio of five students to one computer in 1995, we are nearing our networking goals.

Locally managed information resources have been fully integrated into our school programs. These include the library catalog, a large number of networked CD-ROMs (primarily electronic encyclopedias and full text collections of periodicals), and a range of subject specific CD-ROM titles. These are primary resources specifically selected to support the school curriculum. Online services such as eWorld and other commercial information providers, as well as the Internet, supplement this basic core. The Internet or any online service will not replace these primary resources in the near future.

Our wide area network (WAN) is heavily utilized. Just as with the rest of our technology infrastructure, it continues to evolve in response to users and the changing nature of technologies. We have had to plan for a careful migration to faster network topologies and WAN strategies as demand grows and as services become available. We call this "cooking and growing" the network. This approach has saved us money and headaches, and we have avoided many mistakes. We have been reluctant to invest heavily in any one application or any one service until we have had time to explore and develop it fully. We have taken the same conservative approach to the Internet.

INTERNET ACCESS

In Hampton City Schools, we have not made the Internet the absolute top priority of our program. As our staff has become more attuned to working in networked environments, and as the Internet itself has evolved, we continue to experiment. As we explore options, we have a number of concerns. These questions apply to any telecomputing resource not just the Internet. We wonder how a resource will fit into a school program and into the total mix of information resources available to us. We ask what percentage of our technology budget should be devoted to Internet access? What level of control should we exert over student use of these resources? Who should monitor student use? These are difficult questions and it has not been easy to find answers. Regardless, there is a great deal of public pressure to provide Internet in all classrooms in spite of the questions and the difficulty in answering those questions.

Today we have a variety of ways to reach the Internet. The first three are free once individual computers, modems, and telephone lines are in place. Other approaches are costly either because of hardware requirements or the relatively high cost of connect time the commercial services charge. The NASA Langley program, for example, costs almost $10,000 per school for hardware, and that does not include monthly phone line charges. The InfiNet (local interent service provider) monthly charge is $22 per fifty hours per machine plus phone line costs. Commercial service rates vary but providing access to more than one account is cost prohibitive. Some schools now use the Virginia Department of Education's Electronic Network (VAPEN) while others use PBS/WHRO Television's Learning Link. Another school uses a service provided by Christopher Newport University (Point-to-Point Protocol access or PPP), others use InfiNet (PPP). One school uses the NASA Langley solution. Finally, some have opted to try commercial services such as eWorld, and America Online (AOL) for Internet service. Out of this mix of Internet experiences will come a district-wide strategy for broad-based Internet service for the coming school year.

While VAPEN and Learning Link have been very useful to faculty and staff in understanding telecomputing, they do not offer access to the World Wide Web or provide a graphical user interface. The service from Christopher Newport University is limited and undertaken only for specific projects, so we cannot build a K-12 curriculum around it. Commercial services such as InfiNet and America Online are costly and, in our view, only an interim solution. Of our options, we think we will expand the NASA Langley program significantly in the coming year, but new developments in the Internet service provider community could change that plan. We very much want to find ways to leverage our wide area network to provide service to a much broader segment of our learning community at the lowest possible cost.

In anticipation of using the NASA Langley more widely, we have placed our Information Center staff in UNIX classes to enable them to support Sun UNIX servers in each of their buildings. As we move to a fiber backbone, we can support all UNIX functions centrally and relieve our Information Center staff of this duty. The bandwidth afforded by fiber should also allow all computers on our wide area network, including more than four thousand Macintoshes, access to the Internet from the desktop. For more information on the NASA Langley Internet program, visit http://k12mac.larc.nasa.gov/HPCC_TRS/trs.html

EDUCATION ON THE INTERNET

The District has a long history with telecomputing and the Internet. Through the Virginia Public Education Network (VAPEN), schools have had access to e-mail and other Internet capabilities since 1990.

While VAPEN was designed primarily for teachers and administrators, students were given guest accounts for special projects. Many students also used VAPEN through their teachers' accounts. In 1993, through our PBS affiliate station, WHRO, we achieved a second route to the Internet with Learning Link.

Through these resources, teachers and students in our schools found students and teachers in other states and countries ready to participate in joint projects or in correspondence. Wythe Elementary School teacher Mary Hurst and her third grade class were surprised one day when an Argentinean teacher, with whom they had developed a long term correspondence, showed up in their classroom. The Hampton and the Argentinean classes have shared local histories, lifestyles, and economic facts. The result was broadening for both groups and certainly promoted better global understanding.

Hampton teachers and students have undertaken a number of activities with the Internet. The following are some examples.

- High school students searched for job opportunities posted on the Internet and drew conclusions about which careers were most promising.
- Students involved in the Model United Nations program used the Internet to gather information about their assigned countries from primary sources. They were also able to connect directly to the United Nations and locate the most current data on resolutions passed or under consideration. Some students joined the debate about the European Union, in addition to learning about their assigned country.
- Middle school math students used the Internet to download statistical data for use in a unit on statistics and for use in another project on graphing and charting. They loaded this information onto Microsoft Excel spreadsheets to create graphs and charts. Some used sports statistics, others found information on endangered species. All worked with real data based on specific problems, looking for answers to questions of interest to them.
- High school students worked extensively on the Internet in art history research. Students choose an artist to explore and then search for information about his or her life and work. Some students have included in their results downloaded images from sites such as Le Louvre.
- One class, intrigued by news reports of the appearance of the

red wolf in North Carolina, used the Internet to find out more about wolf species. They discovered via the Internet that the coyote has reintroduced itself widely throughout the lower forty-eight states, including Virginia.

- Since exporting coal is a very significant part of our local economy, one class used the Internet to gather data on coal consumption around the world. An analysis was made of trends that could impact the coal industry and the shipping industry in the United States, especially the Hampton Roads ports, the largest coal exporting center in the world.

- The Internet has become a great source of information about computer ethics, careers in computers, computer related illnesses, and the changes computing brings to society. Susan Brooks, a high school teacher, has collected some of this information and made it available on a student-created home page for Bethel High School at http://www.bethel.hampton. k12.va.us/

- English classes, with teacher Sharon Hurwitz, use the Internet for e-mail, collect graphics for publication, and learn how to put together bibliography entries for data retrieved online.

- When writing to Texas pen pals, one elementary class wanted to know if everyone in the Lone Star State wore cowboy boots and ten gallon hats. According to computer lab director, Darlene Davidson, students who use e-mail and participate in collaborative projects have become very conscious about their language. They don't want to come across to others as "peculiar." Actually one student said she didn't want people in Texas thinking we are a little "weird" because of the way we talk and write.

- An English class used e-mail to explore the topic of racism and why schools need to teach multicultural topics. By posting a question on a LISTSERV and in an America Online conference group, they generated a broad range of responses quickly.

- Phoebus High School brought the Internet into math and science classes. Teacher Mary Stallard used it as means for students to collaborate with scientists at Christopher Newport University, designing habitats for life on Mars and Venus. Sometimes, they engaged in real time chat with scientists. Often they would pose questions or problems for the scientists to consider. Other classes did similar projects with weather information. By downloading daily weather maps over a long period, they were able to develop hypotheses about weather patterns and trends. They then would confer with scientists about their conclusions.

- Using only VAPEN and e-mail, students at Bethel High School have engaged in a project with elementary classes. The high school students play the role of Santa Claus and respond to "Santa" mail from elementary students. It has become an annual ritual and one that the high school students take very seriously.

OTHER TELECOMPUTING AVENUES

Some schools have elected to try other resources such as America Online (AOL) and eWorld. Individual schools have purchased school accounts and provided access time to teachers and students in the Centers for Information Services or one of the school's computer labs. AOL and eWorld have been especially popular with elementary teachers and students, primarily because of their ease of use and organization.

A new dimension of our program will be the Hampton City Schools Bulletin Board, maintained and run by students in each school. It is designed to reach out to citizens who do not have Internet access but who have computers and modems at home. It will also be accessible at a local shopping center where we have set up a touch screen kiosk. The Bulletin Board will also be available on our wide area network. It will play a major role in our language arts program by promoting electronic publishing and electronic discourse.

CONCLUSION

We use the Internet and plan to use it even more in Hampton City Schools. We continue to examine all avenues of access to find the most cost effective solution for our district. We have taken pains to work telecomputing into our school programs and have tried to avoid Internet surfing as an end in and of itself. In these and all other matters related to technology, we continue to learn.

ABOUT THE AUTHOR

Dr. Stallard has worked extensively in both K-12 and higher education as professor, teacher, and administrator. A graduate of both the
University of Virginia and East Tennessee State University, Dr. Stallard
has published widely on the composing process and computers in education. In 1992, he founded the Center for Smart School Development in Norfolk, Virginia. Through the Center, he has worked with
schools and colleges across the country, actively building integrated
information infrastructures. Dr. Stallard can be reached at the Hampton
City Schools, 1819 Nickerson Blvd., Hampton, VA 23663, or phone
(804) 850-5245, or at ckstallard@eworld.com

Part III:

Integrating the Internet with Curriculum

Nine Rules for Using the Internet in Class

David Bell
Teacher
Louisville Junior High School
Louisville, Nebraska

Overview—The Numbers	
Name of School, District or State:	Louisville Public Schools District #34
	Louisville, NE
Number of teachers:	38
Number of students:	452
Grades covered:	K-12
Amount of money in grant or special expenditure (if applicable): n/a	

ABSTRACT

How is the Internet used in the classroom? The Internet is much more than an electronic encyclopedia because it keeps the process of learning alive for students. The Internet demands that teachers change their philosophy, not just the technology they use. To ensure the best results with students, we have to discard old dogmas and relinquish much of our control over the learning process. My first experiences and discoveries in using the Internet in the classroom illustrate how technologies can alter a teacher's classroom philosophy. This article offers nine rules-of-thumb for classroom usage of the Internet.

INTRODUCTION

So, you want to try the Internet in your classroom? You're excited by the idea of active learning. You plan to use your computer as more than an electronic encyclopedia that throws facts at students. Your students are expecting something wonderful, fast, and creative; their parents want something practical and worthy of their tax dollars. You want a new challenge; you want to surf cyberspace.

Get ready to change your mind.

No, don't abandon the idea of using the Internet as a teaching tool. But, be prepared to adjust your thoughts about education. And, especially be prepared to give your students control of what they learn, as frightening as that may sound.

As an old-fashioned teacher, I share most teachers' fear of losing control. I want things done on my terms. My first Internet unit had as many controlling features as any normal lesson. But once the students began using the Internet, old standards of education disintegrated. Daily assignments with firm deadlines could not always be met. Tests over the material were futile because each student was learning different things at different speeds. Students had to be graded on a product instead of a test. Class and time management were chaotic, though productive. After our team of teachers began to laugh at our fretting and gave the students some degree of control over what they learned, we began to see some very practical rules for making the Internet work. I would like to share these rules with you.

RULE ONE: STUDENTS DON'T EXACTLY HAVE TO KNOW WHAT YOU ARE GOING TO TEACH IN ORDER TO LEARN.

My class set out to create a slang dictionary, a project designed to teach the students about linguistics. I'm sure that if I had told the students that we would be using the Internet to study linguistics, they would not have been very excited or motivated to work. So, I saved that vital fact until after we had completed our work on the Internet. We discovered that merely mentioning the word "Internet" meant that students rushed to class. I'm sure our response would not have been as positive if we had substituted "linguistics" for "Internet." This technique may be deceptive, but it works. Emphasize the technology and learning will follow naturally.

RULE TWO: TIME IS VARIABLE AND VALUABLE.

Time is the most monumental problem facing Internet users. It indeed is both variable and valuable. Time problems are constant: you will have to plan around idle breaks, shortages of time or computers, and network or computer downtime. Be sure to have a back-up plan each day.

RULE THREE: THE INTERNET IS ONLY AS FAST AS YOUR (AND AS YOUR RESPONDENTS') EQUIPMENT.

During the initial planning stages, I imagined that everything would be quite speedy. But I discovered that even though the Internet itself may operate rapidly, there are other limiting factors. Everything was slower than I had planned, from sending e-mail to receiving responses from a LISTSERV. But the staff learned to readjust, and back-up plans became mainstays of our lessons. Patience was indeed a virtue with rewards always appearing later. The Internet gave us nearly instantaneous access to people around the world, but they were not able to respond as quickly as we might have expected. Here are several examples.

For our slang survey, we began corresponding with a school in Honolulu, Hawaii. Much of their slang is taken from the old Hawaiian language which our students found fascinating. Even though our school has a direct connection to the Internet, we had to wait over a week for Honolulu's reply. Why? Unlike our school with its own computer lab, our correspondents in Hawaii had just a few computers and a computer club that met only on Mondays after school. So, the other school's facilities undermined the Internet's speed.

We also discovered that sheer geography was a factor in our connections. Although the Internet can bring Australian students and teachers much closer to their U.S. counterparts, their school year is the opposite of ours. Remember basic geography when using the Internet: seasons are completely different from one hemisphere to another. Luckily, we did our unit in February when the Australian schools were just beginning their terms.

RULE FOUR: SUPERVISE YOUR STUDENTS CLOSELY.

If you are planning an Internet unit, all classes will need supervision. Some supervisory problems may develop because some students may have access to the Internet at home. You want to make sure their home-based experience does not cause problems in the classroom. Which leads to another truism: the best part about the Internet is that it is uncensored and the worst part of the Internet is that it is uncensored. Much information on the Internet is quite good, but there's always a need to watch for a few unsavory items. In our case for the school-based computers, the Nebraska State Department of Education filters much of the offensive material. But for many of the Internet connections at home, there are no filters. I always worried about what might appear on our screens.

Teenagers are easy prey for some criminals on the Internet, because students usually are willing to divulge personal information to nearly anyone who asks. Adolescents act often without thinking (perhaps this is one defining attribute of adolescence). Don't give students opportunities to become vulnerable. Our school staff agreed to limit the Internet identifications of students to just their first names. There are no distinguishing characteristics such as physical descriptions, town names, parent names, or other unique tags.

In the course of our project, our students were encouraged to search the Internet for jargon to add to the slang dictionary. Many used class time, outside of normal instruction, to collect words ranging from NASA terminology to Disney cartoons. By team teaching this unit, we always had plenty of supervision in the room. Another supervisory possibility is to use upper level computer students to assist younger students through snags. However, don't always count on older students to make the best decisions. Supervision in one form or another will still be necessary (see Figure 1).

RULE FIVE: USE LISTSERVS AS A WAY TO CONNECT AND CORRESPOND.

How do you find new correspondents and their electronic mail addresses? With whom do you really communicate with in cyberspace? LISTSERVs fill an obvious need in bringing Internet users together, communicating about common problems in spite of differences in time and distance.

Figure 1. Watch your students like a Doberman watches a mail carrier. Your students need to learn netiquette, or simple responsible rules in using the Internet. They also need your supervision for their own safety.

What are LISTSERVs? LISTSERVs are actually mailing lists operating with specially designed software on IBM mainframes. A LISTSERV works likes a magazine subscription; anyone subscribing to a LISTSERV receives copies of messages posted to the LISTSERV server. Many different subscribers will post messages to a specific LISTSERV, dedicated to a specific topic, hoping for a response (see Figure 2).

Questions on a given LISTSERV range widely. Some queries may be about equipment or a situation at school. Others may be looking for a key pal while some are just looking for anything interesting. Try to focus on just one LISTSERV and stick with it. For our project, we

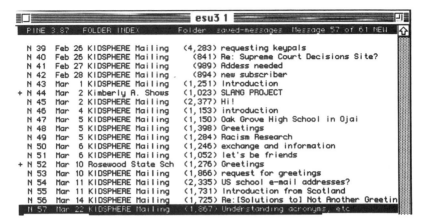

Figure 2. LISTSERVs can be used to find interesting electronic correspondents. A short and eye-catching header for your message to the LISTSERV will help you find readers. In this example from Kidsphere, some headers will stimulate your curiosity, while others will obviously not.

decided to use Kidsphere because of its global subscription base. Kidsphere generates between 30 and 100 messages per day. With that sort of volume, if you can't answer your messages quickly or even bother to empty your electronic in-box, the sheer accumulation of messages will become quite an obstacle.

RULE SIX: IF YOU USE A LISTSERV, MAKE YOUR POSTINGS ATTRACTIVE AND TO THE POINT.

The number of messages distributed on any given LISTSERV is encouraging, but the sheer volume means that many notes are not read. Many subscribers do not bother to open any messages with uninteresting headers or subject descriptors. A descriptor that simply reads "Hello" or "Greetings" does not tell you much about the contents. A subject line that stands out, that specifically defines a topic, such as "Dinosaurs in the Gym," will attract readers. Invent attractive headers for your messages to catch a subscriber's attention. Make a LISTSERV follower want to open your message and read it. Hopefully, your message will generate a reply. In addition, make the process of sending a reply as easy as possible, enhancing the likelihood of answers.

For the slang project, we staged a contest among different groups in the classes. We wanted to avoid flooding the LISTSERV with messages so we concentrated on creating just one posting. To draw attention, this note had to be concise and detailed as well as catchy. The contest was much like those old advertising games: create a slogan in seventeen characters or less. Why seventeen characters? Because Kidsphere would only show the first seventeen characters of a subject line; anything in excess of that length would be truncated from display. With a good header (or slogan), the students constructed a message describing our project, listing an e-mail address, and asking for help. Brevity was also important in the body of the message. LISTSERV subscribers don't bother with messages that are too long. We asked the students to complete the message of the posting in one paragraph. In other words, describe your project in twenty-five words or less.

We had some terrific titles submitted by our students. As moderators of LISTSERVs are very annoyed with headers like "Read this or die" or "Important," we avoided those at any cost. The winning subject line was simply "Young and Slangless." As a measure of its success, it generated instant replies from around the world.

RULE SEVEN: LEARN FROM YOUR MISTAKES.

Our posting to the LISTSERV generated a huge volume of slang words pouring into our account. Responses covered an enormous range of terms. We needed to quickly reduce the number of replies and focus responses on a certain set of categories. A quick survey of our students settled a consensus of five categories. Students wanted slang about money, good, bad, friends, and home. With this redefined focus, students asked for slang that referred just to these terms. After two weeks of collecting e-mail addresses from respondents across the world, we held a class lottery for the most prized addresses. Each group chose two addresses. Addresses from Hawaii, Australia, South Africa, Canada, and California were the ones first selected.

Some of the groups within the classes were more adept at constructing messages than others. The students solved this dilemma by joining forces and composing one generic message for everyone. Then another disaster struck; the network bogged down and the kids couldn't finish the messages within the class period. Again, the students invented a solution by using software to save a copy of the generic message for posting whenever the network was functioning properly.

But even with the mechanics of sending mail settled, we discovered that there were more human problems in securing responses.

For example, given the linguistic nature of the project, I assumed that an academic linguist would welcome an opportunity to communicate with my students. I was wrong. I tried for several days to find a responsive linguistic professor and scholar, but I never received a reply.

On a different and more general scale, we were disappointed with unanswered e-mail. Some who were ardent about participating simply never returned our requests. Yet, we should give them the benefit of the doubt because networks and computers can fail unexpectedly. Faced with this prospect, we certainly recommend that you try to send the same message twice before giving up.

We were surprised by the large number of responses from certain geographic areas such as Canada, Australia, Texas, Michigan, Alaska, and California. But we were equally shocked by the dismal number of responses from other areas, such as the Eastern part of the United States. Some regions simply seem more dedicated to the Internet than others. Replies were uncannily clustered in certain areas. Our survey, while globally widespread, was really confined to certain geographic regions. More contributions from different parts of the United States and from different English-speaking parts of the globe would have been quite welcome.

RULE EIGHT: KEEP YOUR CLASS AND YOUR USE OF THE INTERNET SIMPLE.

E-mail itself is an easy procedure and students pick it up quickly. In our classes, we were not looking for computer proficiency but instead content. A content-driven Internet class means that students need time to explore, to locate Web servers and other Internet resources. The students were not following our neat and organized plans and for some teachers this process caused considerable stress. We observed, though, that students in this process were teaching themselves. By keeping the unit simple, students learned more, not less. The only difference from an ordinary lesson was its lack of structure.

RULE NINE: RELAX, ENJOY YOURSELF, AND ACCEPT CHANGE.

With the students teaching themselves in the course of using the Internet, we found that the teaching staff actually had less to do. Our role became more supervisory and less instructional. As a consequence, both teachers and students enjoyed the process.

RULES REVIEW: SUGGESTED RULES FOR USING THE INTERNET IN YOUR CLASSROOM.

1. Students don't exactly have to know what you are going to teach in order to learn.
2. Time is variable and valuable.
3. The Internet is only as fast as your (and as your respondents') equipment.
4. Supervise your students closely.
5. Use LISTSERVs as a way to connect and correspond.
6. If you use a LISTSERV, make your postings attractive and to the point.
7. Learn from your mistakes.
8. Keep your class and your use of the Internet simple.
9. Relax, enjoy yourself, and accept change.

ABOUT THE AUTHOR

David Bell has taught junior high language arts and reading at the Louisville (NE) Public Schools since 1978. He declares himself officially computer dependent, although he professes to possess more curiosity about the technology than actual skill. He is currently working on another Internet project for his classes. He may be reached by mail at Louisville Public Schools, P. O. Box 489, Louisville, NE 68037-0489; by telephone at (402) 234–3585; or by e-mail to dbell@esu3.esu3.k12.ne.us

Net Gain: Internet Use at New Vista High School

Stevan Kalmon
Teacher
New Vista High School
Boulder, Colorado

Overview—The Numbers	
Name of School, District or State:	New Vista High School Boulder, CO
Number of teachers:	15 FTE (25 including part-time staff)
Number of students:	265
Grades covered:	9-12
Amount of money in grant or special expenditure (if applicable): One grant from Pfizer Corporation of approximately $24,000 to pay for T1 line installation and lease	

ABSTRACT

New Vista High School takes an innovative approach to the Internet by integrating it into daily routines for communication, research, and education. As a new school, New Vista was not burdened with a history of traditional approaches to education and information. This sense of creating history has encouraged students to utilize computers and their connectivity for everyday communications, school activities, and research. As a result, faculty have benefited from student enthusiasm and developed new methodologies.

INTRODUCTION

The national infatuation with the Information Superhighway has made learning to use the Internet a key concept for many technological, industrial, and educational organizations. The Internet presents a fascinating opportunity and challenge for learning—as well as some significant concerns. Internet exploration and experimentation are steps towards essential preparation for the next century and participation in today's increasingly interconnected economy and society. Yet no one knows just where this exploration may lead, which contributes to the fascination, importance, concern, and, more than occasionally, frustration of cyberadventure.

Students and staff at New Vista High School in Boulder, Colorado, began their virtual tour in September 1993 which, not coincidentally, was also the opening date of the school itself. Those involved in creating this small, non-traditional public school recognized that Internet connectivity could play a vital role in providing students with authentic, community-based, and personalized learning experiences. During the planning year that preceded the school's opening, a $24,000 grant was obtained from Pfizer Corporation to purchase a T-1 connection to the Internet and a direct link for every computer at New Vista to the Boulder Valley School District's Internet server. Pfizer supports many educational efforts nationwide through funding. In our case, Valley Labs, a Pfizer subsidiary and Boulder business, was our connection to receiving funding.

In September, 1993, only one member of the New Vista staff (out of fifteen full- and part-time employees) and perhaps a dozen students (out of 125) had Internet experience. The school's only strategy for learning computer and Internet skills was individual curiosity. In the ensuing two years, the formality of our arrangements has not changed substantially, but our experience definitely has. Students and staff have moved from ignorance to Internet awareness by experimentation and regular use. In September, 1995, twenty-six staff members (72 per cent of the staff) have used the Internet. Twenty-one staff (58 per cent) have Internet accounts through the Boulder Valley Internet Project, most of which are used regularly, though not frequently. At least 170 students (65 per cent of the student body) have some Internet experience. Seventy-five students (29 per cent of the total) have acquired Internet accounts, almost all of which are regularly used. In increasing numbers and with greater confidence and purpose, we have been exchanging electronic mail and messages, finding and downloading files from sources throughout the world, constructing our own

Web sites, collaborating on an electronic newspaper, and participating in a number of other activities. As anticipated, these projects have moved from intriguing sidelights to core elements of our curriculum, especially in the languages, social studies, and computer technology. We have entered, and are beginning to settle, a new frontier. Yet, at this stage, we identify that frontier primarily by the activity — by the things that we do here, rather than by the results — the place we are settling. It's an adventure, and after two years, it's just beginning.

A PHILOSOPHY OF COMPUTER TECHNOLOGY

New Vista High School was created by the Boulder Valley School District for the explicit purpose of redefining schooling. Our primary mission is to find meaningful personal connections to learning for each student and staff member. This mission commits us to new strategies for each student, including community experience, respect for and promotion of individual diversity, authentic assessment, and personal paths to graduation. In this context, computer technology and the Internet does not become merely one more required class. Instead, computers are individualized for each student. Students use computer technology for real applications. They make meaningful choices about the use of computer technology by acquiring and demonstrating abilities through contextual learning experiences.

These goals for the students provide the philosophical basis for designing learning strategies. They make explicit particular concerns, including those about the effects of extensive computer use in our society and the importance of context, environment, and authentic work.

Given this philosophy, classes are not absolutely required in computer technology or Internet navigation. Students and staff discover computer and Internet applications in the process of pursuing personal interests. Learning arrangements are primarily tutorial. Those who have more experience, whether staff or students, become the teachers for those who have less Internet knowledge.

Many students and some teachers are fascinated by the technology itself. These are the core of use and tutelage at New Vista. Others discover the utility of a particular computer tool through their own compelling interests. For example, all the students working on the school's magazine learn word processing because it's the only way to get published. Most learn PageMaker to do layout. Many learn

PhotoShop and SuperPaint so that they can put better graphics into the magazine. Publishing on paper, with electronic tools, often leads to virtual publishing. In this case, the magazine appears both in paper and online. Such activities broaden and deepen the skills of everyone and increase an understanding of computer technology.

An important feature of this approach is that teachers learn right along with the students. Frequently, the kids are more adept and more familiar with new software. A teacher's expertise derives not so much from how to use a particular program as it does from when to use one. Student-generated Web sites provide a useful illustration. Few teachers at New Vista are especially proficient with the HyperText Markup Language or HTML, the language that prepares text and files for publication on the World Wide Web. Teachers have become fairly adept, however, at finding reasons for students to construct the sites and, therefore, to learn HTML.

LEARNING ARRANGEMENTS

My own development as an Internet navigator provides a useful example of the New Vista method and of the stages of exploration from ignorance, through awareness, introduction, experimentation, and regular use.

When the school opened in 1993, my only computer experience was word processing on my antique home computer, a ten-year-old IBM XT. Friends and former students had e-mail accounts which intrigued me. With no library in our bare-bones facility, the prospect of online research seemed important. Indeed, as much as anything else, I wanted to relate to the electronic experiences of colleagues and friends.

In December 1993, I acquired an Internet account and sent holiday greetings. On my next log-in to my account about a month later, I had mail to my surprise. Over the course of the next few months, I developed a fairly regular correspondence, mostly with friends, students, and a few other teachers. I created an electronic address book and a large set of folders in which I kept the important messages. I learned primarily by experimentation, trying various operations until something worked. I also learned from my correspondents and a few colleagues at school.

I learned the value of the graphical computer interface, the point-and-click process of working with computers. While graphical commands have become the norm for desktop computers, they have only quite recently gained prominence on the Internet, thanks in large part to the World Wide Web and its browsers. Simplicity in using Internet tools helps a great deal, whatever their form. For example, at New Vista we use Pine, a public domain e-mail system from the University of Washington. Although Pine requires text commands, it lists all the primary commands on the screen. For me, highlighting a message listed on the screen and hitting return, rather than remembering a specific text command, makes a big difference in how quickly I learn. We also use Eudora, an e-mail system that uses straightforward commands very comprehensively. To this day, I still haven't figured out how to handle attachments in Pine but in Eudora, it's simple for me to send and receive files appended to messages.

Currently, I check my mail four or five times a week, spending fifteen minutes to an hour reading and responding to messages. I subscribe to a dozen LISTSERVs, which provide information and commentary about school reform issues, the concerns of Boulder Valley teachers, plans and discussions among the computer and media coordinators in the District, job opportunities, and experiences that might interest students. I look up information at the University of Colorado Library and the Boulder Public Library by logging in from school. I could conduct my research worldwide. Using Netscape, I browse the Web looking for useful information and notions, creative displays, and interesting sites to share, and to develop an overall sense of what's possible since I coordinate student efforts on the Web server.

Like me, almost all the staff and students have learned primarily in informal ways. But we have started to use organized classes and training sessions. The Boulder Valley Internet Project (http://bvsd.k12.co.us) provides an extensive training program for teachers. During our second year, a few of our staff have used these sessions to learn about new systems or applications. We have also provided students with occasional classes on using the Internet and publishing on the World Wide Web. There's also a connection with the Center for LifeLong Learning and Design (L3D Center), part of the Computer Engineering Department at the University of Colorado. Through the L3D Center, we are learning to use computers and the Internet more effectively.

In 1995-96, we will conduct a year-long student construction project on the World Wide Web with each student's participation ranging from a quarter of the academic year to the entire year. Participants will meet once a week for three hours, substantially expanding and improving the school's site while acquiring significant experience and skills with computer and Internet applications. We will also offer a programming class. We anticipate that more staff will include the Internet in their courses. There will be a weekly computer workshop for staff, providing tutoring in specific applications and assistance in ongoing projects. In addition, we will continue and deepen our connection with the L3D Center.

EXAMPLES OF CURRENT USE

The New Vista community makes varied and highly individualistic use of the Internet, but certain activities reflect our use especially well.

Electronic Mail and Talk

Nearly every individual with an Internet account at New Vista sends and receives e-mail. That activity accounts for the largest use of the Internet at the school. Students also talk to each other and to others around the world virtually. Many students prefer the immediacy of virtual talk, scanning the District network for a chance to start a virtual conversation with almost anyone online. Indeed, if you log on any time between eight in the morning to four in the afternoon, you will almost certainly get talk queries from several students throughout the District.

Some educators disapprove of the use of the Internet for social activities. Virtual talk on the Internet resembles note passing in class more than serious educational business. Our District prohibits students from creating chat servers or Multi-User Domains (MUDs), which provide scenarios for fantasy-based dialogues. Even Web-based student directories are frowned upon. These restrictions are based in part on legitimate concerns about preserving scarce bandwidth resources.

While such chat may not meet explicit curricular expectations, it provides significant learning benefits. First, it extends the walls of the classroom. Students participate in a larger community, not just other students in the school but correspondents in the vast territory of cyberspace. Second, the inherent appeal of such activity to students encourages many to use computers, especially those who would not otherwise do so. Once engaged by electronic conversation, students usually graduate to more serious digital exercises. Thanks to this process, some of our most expert computer users are kids who don't fit the "techie" profile. Third, in mastering electronic tools involved in these exchanges, students teach other students how to use software and hardware. Students share their expertise and strategies with other students, not for a mere academic goal, but for the very real purpose of conversation and play.

Staff use of e-mail has been more limited. A few staff have extensive contacts through individual messages and subscriptions to specific LISTSERVs and newsgroups. Internet connectivity is gradually working its way into the classroom. For example, a geography teacher has students make e-mail connections with students in the regions that they're studying. The bicycle shop teacher has helped students establish an extensive network of consultants to help with repairs and business development. But many staff have not found the time to explore this medium seriously. Consequently, classroom use of e-mail, whether for communication with other classrooms or with professionals studying similar material or issues, remains largely untapped. We expect that more training and experience will encourage staff members to make more use of this tool.

Research

Access to the Internet has enabled New Vista students to carry out research in new ways. Students use the Internet to connect to the online catalogs at both the Boulder Public and University of Colorado Libraries. They also connect to information summaries and databases posted by libraries around the country. Since the school does not have a library of its own, these virtual libraries in effect collectively become New Vista's library. Internet browsing and indexing have become fundamental methods of research. The physical trip to the library only occurs so that students can check out the books and periodicals that they have found in their virtual excursions. School-based electronic searches in turn have become a natural part of classes and instruction. Students search the Internet for information on topics of interest. Although there is no required class in the use of Internet tools, such as WAIS, Veronica, and Fetch, many students at New Vista have learned how to use them simply because they find the process fascinating.

However, students and staff have discovered that the Internet-based information can be limited and difficult to uncover. For example, some Web servers exist merely to provide corporate or institutional presence on the Internet, a form of commercial promotion without providing much useful information. While some Web sites provide useful resources, finding useful Internet-based information is not guaranteed because even search engines like WebCrawler and Yahoo do not comprehensively index the Web in the way that a good card catalogue provides an exact summary of a library's holdings.

While the potential of the Internet as a source of information seems limitless, more of its infrastructure needs to be developed before that potential can be realized. Consequently, at New Vista we have focused on the kinds of uses that seem most appropriate to the current interests of our community. Some conduct virtual interviews and surveys while others pursue specific areas, such as images of planets and stars or digital weather maps. Working with the L3D Center, students and staff are exploring ways to improve the usefulness of the Web as a research tool. In these ways, New Vista students are not only using available tools but also contributing to its overall development.

World Wide Web browsers: Mosaic and Netscape

In less than two years, Mosaic and Netscape have transformed the Internet. Their graphical interfaces have dramatically eased navigation and publication on the Internet. Students at New Vista have been immediately and powerfully attracted to Internet publishing, creating individual home pages, sites for school enterprises such as the Bike Lab, AMISH (Auto Mechanics on the Information Superhighway), and the World Peas Cafe. Student interest has largely driven these efforts with students recruiting faculty to teach classes on Web publishing. In these classes, students learn the HyperText Markup Language in order to create their own Web pages. HTML provides the vehicle for students to master both computer technology and the processes of work and learning.

Students are already beginning to explore enhancements such as the Virtual Reality Markup Language, or VRML; Common Graphic Interface or CGI scripts for creating interactive pages; and Java, a new Internet authoring tool. Beyond learning about these tools, students also learn about the creative process itself and how to evaluate the work of others.

FUTURE DIRECTIONS

After two years of direct connectivity, we are just beginning to discover the educational benefits and challenges of the Internet. We plan to expand Internet use through professional networking; electronically linked projects and student exchanges; construction of an electronic library; and an improved connection to research and teaching at the

University of Colorado. Students will navigate the Internet to learn about colleges and other opportunities they might pursue after high school. All of these applications require that learning is based on real student interest and work rather than abstract motivation.

Substantial concerns still exist such as developing genuine computer literacy and overcoming many inefficiencies in using the Internet for research and learning. We believe, however, that direct and reflective participation in this environment provides the most effective means to respond to these concerns. In order to understand this medium, you have to experience it. We consider ourselves quite fortunate to have this opportunity to work on the information superhighway at the very moment it is being constructed, exploring virtual regions as they become available. We are discovering first-hand what the information society is and will be.

ABOUT THE AUTHOR

Stevan Kalmon is a language arts and social studies teacher at the New Vista High School in Boulder, Colorado. He directs the publication of the student magazine and coordinates the school's computer technology efforts. He is also involved with the Center for LifeLong Learning and Design at the University of Colorado, serving as a liaison between the Center and the school. Before joining the New Vista staff, he worked on several education reform projects, including the design of a progressive charter school for the Oakland (California) Unified School District. Stevan can be contacted at New Vista High School, 805 Gillaspie Dr., Boulder, CO 80301 (303) 447-5401 or send electronic mail to kalmon@bvsd.k12.co.us

Jazz Up your Curriculum with Global SchoolNet Telecommunications Projects

Lorna Pasos
Project Coordinator
"Where On the Globe is Roger?" and "Geogame"
Global SchoolNet Foundation
El Cajon, California

Overview—The Numbers	
Name of School, District or State:	Pacoima Elementary Los Angeles Unified School District Los Angeles, CA
Number of teachers:	60
Number of students:	1,500
Grades covered:	K-6
Amount of money in grant or special expenditure (if applicable): n/a	

ABSTRACT

Several successful Internet projects have been developed by the Global SchoolNet Foundation including "Where On the Globe is Roger?" and "Geogame." Other efforts by the Foundation are known as "Newsday," "Family Tree-Mail," and "Fieldtrips." They have been used in classes for several years and have proven to be very popular and effective with students. In addition, the Foundation's LISTSERV, dedicated to K-12 education, encourages the use of the Internet in schools by linking teachers and others together electronically.

ABOUT THE GLOBAL SCHOOLNET FOUNDATION

The Global SchoolNet Foundation, dedicated to K-12 education, was formerly known as the FrEdMail Foundation. FrEd is an abbreviation of Free Education. The current Foundation continues this tradition by not charging any fees for its projects. This practice was originally created by Al Rogers and a large group of dedicated volunteers involved in the original set-up of the FrEdMail bulletin boards, which are still operational. Al Rogers has been recognized for his contributions, most recently at the Conference known as Tel-Ed '94 where he received the ISTE Distinguished Service Award.

The Foundation's newsgroups, found on many readers, are read by educational staff and volunteers around the world. These newsgroups follow a strict code of ethics and violation of this code means loss of access. This code and the moderation of the Foundation's newsgroups and bulletin boards makes them a popular medium in classrooms.

The Foundation supports a high level of service to teachers and students around the world. For example, the LISTSERV "Hilites" is one of the oldest LISTSERVs dedicated to classroom learning projects. It is moderated so postings meet the Foundation's strict criteria. It is reserved just for K-12 teachers. To subscribe, send a message to majordomo@gsn.org Leave the subject line blank, and type in the body of the note, "subscribe Hilites."

Let's examine some of the Foundation's specific projects.

WHERE ON THE GLOBE IS ROGER?

Is geography boring to your students? Are you having trouble finding a way to motivate them to write about geographical topics? The project known as *Where On the Globe is Roger?* can change those reactions. Designed for students in grades four through eight, it specifically meets the needs of teachers in subject areas as diverse as the language arts, social sciences, and even basic math. This project began in 1994 and will continue at least through 1996.

Roger, the central figure of the project, is a real person. Roger Williams, a former U. S. Marine Corps combat pilot and retired airline pilot, is in the midst of realizing his dream of driving around the world. He invites students to travel along with him vicariously over the Internet. In 1994, he drove his 1982 Dodge truck from the United States through Mexico, central America, and South America, all the way to Tierra del Fuego. From Brazil, he shipped his truck to Australia where he spent seven months exploring this continent in the southern hemisphere. In early 1995, he moved on to Japan, driving for some four months in the islands. In July 1995, he headed with his truck to Vladivostok, Russia where he traveled westward. Plans are taking shape for travel in Europe as well as Africa. During these excursions, Roger visits schools and educational groups, meeting with students and teachers, and sending reports back electronically to all participants in the project.

Roger Williams contacted the Global SchoolNet Foundation in 1994 asking if we could help him contact schools in the course of his travels. His idea was to promote international communication between children from different countries on his expedition. He hopes that by encouraging electronic communication among students and teachers he will "somehow enable them to find a better way to deal with problems in the future rather than resorting to armed conflict."

This project is a low-response telecommunications project, in that it requires just an electronic address and registration to receive reports from Roger. Participants in the project can use their connections to enhance and customize the project as they see fit. Some students and teachers have written directly to Roger, others have sent classroom biographies, while still others have used opportunities to establish penpals, take part in curriculum projects, and simply ask questions.

For those classes just beginning to use the Internet, this project is an excellent chance to start learning more about the global reach of electronic communication. Further details on this and other projects can be found at the foundation's home page, at http://www.gsn.org (see Figure 1). On the home page, all of the reports by Roger, a Frequently Asked Questions (FAQ) file, a list of schools with electronic addresses that have been following Roger, reports from schools that Roger has visited, and other details are available.

GEOGAME

If your students still think that longitude and latitude, time zones, land forms, and rivers are worthless, here's a different kind of Internet project that will help them learn geographic details and really enjoy it.

As a retired teacher, I casually asked Al Rogers if there was some way I could help with the Foundation and the Internet. He suggested that I moderate "Geogame," originally invented by Tom Clauset of Winston-Salem, North Carolina and managed by the Foundation since 1992. I really didn't know what I was getting into. "Geogame" started with just forty participants. Now there are over 200 involved in it, in three cycles a year in the autumn, winter, and spring.

"Geogame" requires a moderate level of responses and interactivity from its participants. Those joining the project provide geographic information about their own community and also answer a questionnaire. When the game sections are sent out, students solve a match-up portion and send their answers back to be corrected and tabulated.

Jane Moore, a teacher in Winnetka, Illinois, found that her fifth graders were completely entranced by "Geogame." She saw students ready to use atlases, gazetteers, road atlases, biographical dictionaries, and maps in the school library to decipher the clues. She also noted that the students themselves were proud of their efforts in solving the geographical questions, and looked forward to a new round of "Geogame" queries. Christa Fagnant, a fourth grader in Alaska, found the game exciting. It also provided an opportunity for her and her classmates to use all sorts of materials such as road maps to solve specific questions.

This project is an excellent one to introduce students to Internet exploration. It is based on e-mail but can also be completed on dis-

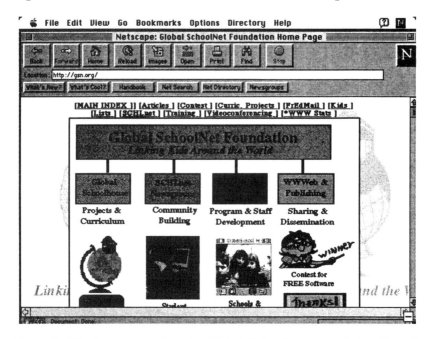

Figure 1. The home page for the Global SchoolNet Foundation (http://www.gsn.org) provides descriptions of all the Foundation's projects and activities for K-12 students and educators.

kette outside the classroom. "Geogame" is designed to address curriculum needs in geography, language arts, math, and multicultural education as well as give students an opportunity to do research. For more information send a message to geogame@gsn.org

NEWSDAY

Would you like your students to gather news and compile a newspaper? "Newsday" may be just the project for your language arts or journalism class. It requires a large number of electronic responses and much more class time than previously mentioned projects.

"Newsday" works by making each registered class responsible for a specific number of articles about their class, school, and geographical area. These articles are then collected and sent to other schools participating in the project, much like the Associated Press sends stories to its subscribers. Students read the "Newsday" releases and decide which to use and edit in their own newspapers. With this project, students become news gatherers and reporters, editors, layout and graphic artists, and eventually publishers.

Participation in this project, on a national and international scale, leads to an understanding of broad issues that transcends local events. It can involve students in weeks of cross-cultural activity. Schools may use several techniques actually to produce the newspapers, from simple mockups with word processors to sophisticated layouts with desktop publishing programs. When the newspaper is printed, each participating school is required to send a copy of the newspaper to all of the participating schools and to the Foundation. These newspapers often stimulate interesting discussions among students over which articles were chosen, why they may have been picked, and how they were edited.

"Newsday" specifically addresses the needs of classes in the language arts and journalism. The wide range of possible stories means that other disciplines could be involved in the project as well. For more information, send a message to newsday@gsn.org

FAMILY TREE-MAIL

Family Tree-Mail was initiated in 1995 on a limited trial, coordinated through the Global SchoolHouse at Jefferson Junior High School in Oceanside, California. This unique project takes advantage of Globalink's "Language Assistant" translation software to allow students who speak languages other than English, such as Spanish, French, Italian, and German, to meet and write. Anthologies are then created and shared with all participants.

This project encourages correspondence among students in foreign languages, helps to develop dialogues between different cultural groups, and improves skills in reading and composition. Updates on this project can be obtained by sending a message to majordomo@gsn.org In the body of this note, type "subscribe treemail–watch" and your name.

FIELDTRIPS

"Fieldtrips" gives students a chance to exchange information about specific field trips and excursions to different museums, institutions, and other sites with other students over the Internet. It provides a ready audience for reports and summaries of visits to local sights. Before a field trip, students post an electronic announcement about their excursion. Members of the project ask questions over the Internet related to the journey and students on the actual field trip try to answer all queries as part of the trip. Students on the actual field trip are requested to answer specific questions and report back digitally on the list. As a result, students on real field trips are very motivated as observers and reporters to their electronic colleagues. To subscribe, send a message to majordomo@gsn.org with nothing in the subject line. Write simply subscribe "fieldtrips-L"

OTHER EFFORTS

The Foundation supports other projects including "Scientist On-Tap," "Ask a Geologist," "Global Grocery List," and "The Jason Project." To learn more about them, visit the Foundation's home page at http://www.gsn.org All of the Foundation's projects promise greater practical use of the Internet as an educational resource, at its most elementary level with e-mail. These projects link together diverse audiences around the world to simply communicate and learn from each other. Their effectiveness with the young prove the value of the Internet as an educational medium now and well into the future.

ABOUT THE AUTHOR

Five years ago, Lorna Pasos retired from the Los Angeles Unified School District after a career spanning three decades in the elementary grades K-6. Lorna also taught students with learning handicaps. In retirement, Lorna is an Educational Consultant for "Where On the Globe is Roger?" and serves as sysop for the FrEdMail bulletin board for the Cajon Valley Union School District. A member of the Board of Directors of the Global SchoolNet Foundation, Lorna also manages the "Geogame" project. Mail will reach Lorna at 1903 East Chase Avenue, El Cajon, CA 92020 or phone (619) 444–3033, or send e-mail to lpasos@gsn.org

Surfing the Internet in Santa Cruz

Jory Post
Teacher
Happy Valley School
Santa Cruz, California

Overview—The Numbers	
Name of School, District or State:	Happy Valley School Happy Valley School District Santa Cruz, CA
Number of teachers:	6
Number of students:	150
Grades covered:	K-6

Amount of money in grant or special expenditure (if applicable):
Received a number of grants which were used in parts for the projects. Amounts include $15,000 SB-1510 California Technology Grant; $7,000 from California Educational Initiative Funds for TOWS; and $12,000 GATE California Gifted and Talented Education Grant for two years.

ABSTRACT

The success of the Internet in Santa Cruz's Happy Valley School is due in large part to the collaboration of teachers, parents, and students on several projects. In addition, there has been additional support for specific projects that range from the cultivation of electronic pen pals to creative writing to virtual investing and imaginary electronic travel. With the use of the World Wide Web, we expect students will find even more opportunities to take advantage of electronic resources from their desktop computers all around the world.

INTRODUCTION

With sledge hammers ready, a handful of Happy Valley staff members and parents, myself included, converged on the school kitchen on the first Saturday of spring break in 1993. By the end of the week, we had designed, built, painted, wired, and stocked a computer lab with five Apple Macintosh LC computers.

Nestled in the foothills of the Santa Cruz Mountains four miles from the Pacific Ocean and the famous Steamers Lane surfing spot, Happy Valley School is home to 150 students and five classroom teachers. Two years after the creation of this computer lab, Happy Valley students are now surfing the Internet with twenty Macintosh computers and a direct Frame-Relay connection.

The expeditious success of Happy Valley's technology program can be attributed to a number of sources. Primarily, staff members, along with representatives of the Parents' Club, had an understanding of the importance of technology in general, and telecommunications specifically. Fund raisers were held, cars were sold, and personal contributions were made to ensure that Happy Valley students had access to technology connecting them to the world.

A number of grants were also written and procured. A grant of $7,000 from the California Educational Initiatives Fund supported the development of an online literary magazine for fourth through sixth grade students around the country. A $15,000 award from the 1994 SB-1510 California Technology Grant helped to develop telecommunication stations and support staff development in both multimedia and telecommunications. Through a regional CalRen grant, Happy Valley received from Pacific Bell a direct Frame-Relay connection, transmitting information at speeds in our case at 128,000 bits per second.

Two other grants were implemented for the 1995-96 school year. The Gifted and Talented Education Grant from California provides $24,000 over the next two years. With it, every classroom in Happy Valley will receive four hours per week of computer lab instruction, much of it dedicated to telecommunications. In addition, I have received a Christa McAuliffe Fellowship Award to develop virtual field trips for students and teachers throughout the Monterey Bay region.

ELECTRONIC PEN PALS

Let's examine some of the school's specific electronic projects. Our first leap into the Internet involved a digital pen pal project, using the Project Bulletin Boards in the Electronic Schoolhouse on America Online (keyword=ESH). With these bulletin boards, we were able to find the names and addresses of schools and teachers interested in pen pal partners.

After making initial contact with teachers through e-mail, class lists were shared and students were paired. All students in grades three through six were given at least two pen pals, and in some cases, three. Our partner schools were St. Margaret-Mary in Chicago, Peck Place in Orange Grove, Connecticut, and Mt. Tamalpais in San Francisco, California. Students were encouraged to write at least four paragraphs in each letter. The paragraphs focused on personal biographies, description of classes, Happy Valley, and Santa Cruz.

CHAT ROOMS

As an extension of this effort, we discovered chat rooms on America Online (AOL) as well as Internet Relay Chat (IRC). In addition to ongoing communications, e-mail students participated in live discussions with their pen pals. Some chats were open-ended and students were allowed some freedom in their electronic conversations. With St. Margaret-Mary School in Chicago, we established specific parameters for discussions to maintain focus.

After becoming familiar with the idiosyncrasies and etiquette of chat rooms, we allowed students to spend more time online without specific parameters. We identified a few online rooms that we felt were "safe." However, we always recorded all conversations that students had online. This log helped to ensure the use of appropriate language and content on both sides of the conversation. There were rare occasions when a student would use abusive language and we learned quickly how to handle these situations. We also discovered that most chat rooms include a function that allows you to ignore others in the room. With this option, their conversations do not appear on the screen (see Figure 1).

This experimental foray into real-time telecommunications led our students all over the country, meeting students, teachers, and community members. With a growing understanding of this technology, we began to track our contacts geographically with a map of the United States next to the computer and modem. New guidelines required that any student working online had to ask the geographic locations of the participants in their chat rooms. Within a week of starting this assignment, our map had over eighty pins from coast to coast.

Figure 1. Students participate in a live chat with students at another school.

COLLEGIALITY

As we continued to use the Internet, we discovered greater uses for it in the classroom. As we introduced students to it and developed sensible curricular applications, we began to see the value of the Internet as a teaching tool. Since Happy Valley is a small school with one sixth grade teacher (me), the opportunity for regular discussion and brainstorming with peers has been minimal. That all changed as a result of the Internet. I first posted a few messages on educational bulletin boards and began to receive mail from teachers interested in similar issues. From these initial contacts, I would meet online with teachers in private chat rooms for more detailed discussions.

The most noteworthy contact that I made was with Leni Donlan of the Town School for Boys. Leni and I met in a chat room and proceeded to have an eight-month online conversation. This dialogue moved from discussion of educational philosophy to plans for a nationwide online curriculum project. Our virtual encounter led us to create, post, and operate a stock market simulation called Taking Stock.

TAKING STOCK

Taking Stock proved the value of simulation projects for students on the Internet. It was thematic in nature, encouraging the integration of skills across the curriculum. It taught students and teachers about the stock market, but more importantly, it demonstrated how to use telecommunications in a meaningful way.

My joint fifth and sixth grade class at Happy Valley acted as the test site for much of the activities of Taking Stock. I designed six activities and accompanying worksheets for the project, focusing on converting fractions and decimals to money, researching corporations on the Internet, writing and sharing persuasive letters, and understanding stock symbols. In the project, students all over the country received cash credits for completing worksheets correctly. They were allowed to use these cash credits for purchasing stocks (see Figure 2).

Thirty teachers from across the country signed up nearly 800 students for the first year of Taking Stock. They learned about the project on America Online and downloaded activities from AOL's Electronic Schoolhouse. Teachers divided their classes into groups containing just three or four students each. Leni and I then took these 250 groups

Figure 2. Students work on a fraction activity in the Internet project, Taking Stock.

and created fifty-four investment teams. Each team had members from five different schools across the country. Team composition was posted along with e-mail addresses so team members could share messages and meet in chat rooms.

Before purchasing stocks, team members were required to send each other persuasive letters, trying to convince others to purchase a specific stock. The team could only purchase stocks for which persuasive letters had been written. Once all letters had been posted and read, the team members voted on which stocks to purchase.

We discovered that time zone differences had a negative effect on chat possibilities. In the 1995-96 version of the project, we have made adjustments to compensate for time zones and other problems. The project can be found in the Electronic Schoolhouse on America Online, or at the Taking Stock site at http://www.santacruz.k12.ca.us/~jpost/projects/TS/TS.html

TOWS: THE ONLINE WRITE STUFF

Another project developed at Happy Valley School is known as *TOWS*, or *The Online Write Stuff*. TOWS is an online literary magazine written by and for fourth through sixth graders. It is an extension of a local magazine called *The Write Stuff*. Through *TOWS*, any fourth through sixth grade student in the world may submit their writing to us for potential publication. The only guidelines are that materials must be submitted electronically and they must be appropriate for a fourth through sixth grade audience. Fiction, poetry, songs, book and movie reviews, essays, and memoirs are all possible submissions for *TOWS*. (See Figure 3.)

Last year, four issues of *TOWS* were published online, including contributions from fifteen students. Students received cash prizes for their published submission, with fifty dollars for first place, twenty-five dollars for second place, fifteen dollars for third place, ten dollars for fourth place, and eleven five dollar, fifth place prizes. The first year the prize money came from the California Education Initiative Fund. In subsequent years, it is from donations by individuals, schools, and local businesses. My fifth and sixth grade students acted as editors, reviewers, word processors, and distributors of this literary magazine. Five issues of *TOWS* appeared during the 1995–96 school year, beginning in October and ending in May. Any fourth through sixth grade student may submit their work by sending it to TOWS4Kids@aol.com

Figure 3. TOWS submissions are edited by Happy Valley students in the school's computer lab.

THE WORLD WIDE WEB

The World Wide Web and its browsers, such as Netscape, have turned many cumbersome Internet processes into exciting and motivational educational exercises. From the CIA World Factbook to the White House to Uncle Bob's Kids Page, the World Wide Web offers educators and students access to many resources. For example, at one time Happy Valley students clustered into small groups to read the local newspaper each morning and give, eventually, reports on their findings. Now, those same groups have online access to newspapers from around the world and give up-to-the-minute reports on their discoveries. Students also access news in proprietary services from AOL, Prodigy, CompuServe, and eWorld. They use Web-based search engines to find topics of interest or specific newspapers (see Figure 4).

Students used to turn in a written report or read their findings to the class; now they use HyperStudio or other programs to create multimedia reports. Using the Interact simulation Caravans, students in my classroom study countries of the world and make oral and multimedia presentations to the class. In addition to using printed materials, students go online to search electronic encyclopedias or cruise the

Web to find resources such as the *CIA World Factbook*. Students also use Web servers to gather information about flags, currency, cultural styles, and current events.

A particularly interesting activity, written by Marilyn Burns, is called Travel Agent. It takes a whole new approach with students and the Internet. With it, students design a trip and create an itinerary, compile a budget, and construct a report about the trip. The Web provides a host of related sites, including The Virtual Tourist, that assist students in putting their trips together.

The World Wide Web has also given us the opportunity to create a worldwide presence on the Internet for our school. Located at http://www.happy-valley.hvsd.k12.ca.us, the Happy Valley home page includes information on projects such as Taking Stock, *TOWS*, *The Write Stuff*, and much more. In addition, some students have developed their own personal home pages which are attached to the school home page.

THE FUTURE

While the power of information retrieval through the World Wide Web becomes strikingly apparent to all who use it, the reality remains that only a small percentage of teachers and an even smaller percentage of students have access to this technology. Prior to the current

Figure 4. The Happy Valley School can be found on the World Wide Web at http://www.happy-valley.hvsd.k12.ca.us

telecommunications boom, the issue of equity of access to information and resources has never been widely acknowledged. The gap between well-endowed schools and those with less resources continues to grow. The appearance of high-speed telecommunications capabilities in schools offers an opportunity to narrow that gap. Success will require a conscious effort to share resources or this gap could grow even wider. It is incumbent upon those with knowledge and skills to share with others and make it a priority to strive for equity of access for all.

As a personal example, I am creating and assisting others in the development of virtual field trips on the World Wide Web. My primary goal is to make these exercises meaningful and interactive, which students and teachers everywhere can use with ease. Students at Happy Valley will test these field trips known as Sliding through Spain, Happy Valley Virtual Gallery, Long Marine Lab, the Virtual Telescope, and many more. The home page for these can be found at http://www.santacruz.k12.ca.us/~jpost/vft/

The staff and community of Happy Valley School have made a commitment to pursue telecommunications as a means to fulfill our curriculum goals. As we look to the future, we see a continuation of our current activities and an expansion of our Web presence. We plan to develop more resources not only for our own students but for teachers and students throughout the world.

ABOUT THE AUTHOR

Jory Post is an educator and author, teaching fifth and sixth grade classes at Happy Valley School since 1976. He is also the technology coordinator and mentor teacher for the District. Jory has received several grants for technology projects most recently including the 1995-96 Christa McAuliffe Fellowship Award. His project, Virtual Field Trips of Monterey Bay, can be found at http://www.santacruz.k12.ca.us/~jpost/vft/. Post has written or co-written several books including *Living in a Family, Stopping Violence, Learning About AIDS*, and *Communication for a Livable World*.

Part IV:

Publishing on the Web

Vocal Point: *A Collaborative, Student Run Online Newspaper**

Scott Dixon
Teacher
Centennial Middle School
Boulder, Colorado

and

Libby Black
Director
Boulder Valley Internet Project
Boulder, Colorado

Overview—The Numbers	
Name of School, District or State:	Centennial Middle School Boulder Valley School District Boulder, CO
Number of teachers:	~35 in the school; ~1,500 in the district
Number of students:	~600 in the school; ~25,000 in the district
Grades covered:	6-8 in the school, K-12 in the district
Amount of money in grant or special expenditure (if applicable): n/a	

ABSTRACT

Vocal Point is a collaborative, online electronic newspaper published on the World Wide Web. This project, which demonstrates the power of the Internet as a tool for teachers and

---

*Illustrations reprinted with permission of the authors and their respective schools.

learners, began as a middle school publications class project at Centennial Middle School in Boulder, Colorado. In June 1994, with the help of a local scientist and a graduate journalism student, Vocal Point *became the first collaborative student newspaper on the World Wide Web. Students at Centennial collaborated electronically with high school students in the community and around the United States to produce an issues-oriented publication. All of the writing, design, and production for* Vocal Point *is done by students. During the summer of 1995, an issue of the newspaper was created by students in Colorado, Minnesota, and Illinois.*

INTRODUCTION

June, 1994 marked the arrival of one of the world's first collaborative, student online newspaper, *Vocal Point*, on the World Wide Web. It is the creative product of a middle school publications class that incorporates the talents of graduate students in the University of Colorado School of Journalism, a software engineer at the National Center for Atmospheric Research, the Knight Ridder Information Design Lab, and journalism students from a local high school.

Since its inception, this online electronic newspaper has grown into a monthly publication conceived, designed, and created by students in grades six through twelve from around the country. *Vocal Point* is unique for several reasons. For example, students learn to work independently as well as collaboratively. As a class they reach consensus on topics and the assignment of individual roles. As individuals, they learn from the students who had their role before them, and act as mentors for the students after them (see Figure 1).

Perhaps the most powerful attribute of this educational project is that the participating students have been empowered and motivated

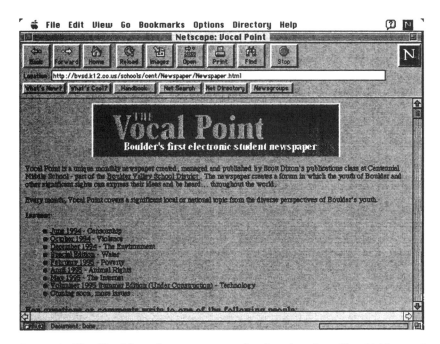

Figure 1. The *Vocal Point* home page can be found at http://bvsd.k12.co.us/schools/cent/Newspaper/Newspaper.html

to be learners, teachers, and leaders. That this project is in the form of an electronic newspaper is not accidental; newspapers are natural forums for both communication and learning. The Internet also can be harnessed to catalyze similar learning opportunities for students in many "subject areas" and all grade levels.

We will share with you the evolution and process of this project. We will also reflect, with input from students, on the key components of the project and the critical pieces which have enabled the students to make this project their own. We hope that our description will highlight some of the factors which make the Internet such a powerful educational tool. We hope in turn to help other teachers capitalize on the lessons we have learned.

THE INTERNET COMES TO CENTENNIAL MIDDLE SCHOOL

In Autumn 1992, the computer laboratory at Centennial Middle School in Boulder, Colorado was connected to the Internet as part of a three-school pilot project sponsored by the National Science Foundation, the University of Colorado, and the Boulder Valley School District.

In the belief that access to the Internet and its vast array of resources would be of great benefit to education now and in the future, a plan was developed to allow individual access to the Internet for every student and teacher. A contract, clearly stating the responsibilities and etiquette associated with Internet access, was developed to ensure proper use of this resource. The idea was to empower and trust the user with individual access, while emphasizing the responsibilities inherent in its use.

Computer classes began to take advantage of the Internet connection immediately. The nature of the school's Internet connection allowed each student to claim a personal account. As excitement about the resources on the Internet spread throughout the school, students clamored for their personal accounts. They took time from their lunch breaks or dropped in after school, just to learn how to use the Internet.

Some students began to experiment and learn more about the Internet in sessions of Centennial's Computer Club, which met every Friday after school. There, Scott Dixon of Centennial and Joe Vanandel, a community volunteer and software engineer for the National Center for Atmospheric Research, and the students explored the Internet. In these meetings, students discovered the World Wide

Web and the HyperText Markup Language or HTML, the Web's authoring language.

Fortuitously, several of the Computer Club students were also in Scott's publications class. It was a natural jump to move from desktop publishing to Internet publishing.

VOCAL POINT IS BORN

With the help of Jill Tucker, a University of Colorado graduate student in the School of Journalism, the publications class was redesigned. Students assumed roles in this re-organization just like those similar in any professional media group. Positions were created for news editors, copy editors, graphic artists, photographers, HTML programmers, researchers, and writers. Centennial students collaborated with an interested group of journalism students from a local high school. Through e-mail, students and teachers selected censorship as the theme for *Vocal Point's* first issue. This theme provided the first opportunity for teachers and students to negotiate the parameters of leadership and responsibility in terms of this new medium, an online newspaper, for an unknown but assumedly diverse audience.

Each student, as an effective member of the publications team, was required to engage in both independent and cooperative learning. For example, the news editor drew up timelines and set dates to distribute tasks and balance work loads. The graphic artist learned how to use a scanner and photograph editing software in order to manipulate images. The HTML programmer had to learn how to download technical documents and utilities from Internet sites. Using these Internet sites as models, the programmers were able to learn the Hypertext Markup language (HTML) necessary to put *Vocal Point* online. Once the student photographers, researchers, writers, and graphic artists completed their respective tasks, the HTML programmers converted these various documents into the formats necessary for electronic presentation.

The first issue of *Vocal Point* appeared on the World Wide Web in June, 1994. We believe it was the first student newspaper of its kind in the world. The students involved in *Vocal Point* went beyond being simply consumers of information and became information producers and providers. Going beyond just publishing what they researched, the students added hypertext pointers to other Web sites, with additional reference information on keywords within their stories. This feature enables *Vocal Point* readers to access extensive factual information beyond the original story.

VOCAL POINT EVOLVES

Sometimes great projects are inspired by one chance meeting. Such was the case with the evolution of *Vocal Point*.

In April, 1994, the Boulder Valley Schools were visited by a group of Japanese business people. They included the Centennial Middle School on their tour. This visit led to a story appearing in the Japanese newspaper *Asahi*, which some call the Japanese equivalent of the *New York Times*. A representative for a Japanese distance-based education company, Kawaijuku, saw the article and followed with a visit to the school in August. Shigefumi Murata, Chief Representative for Kawaijuku, came to Boulder to discuss advance plans for a visit in October when several Japanese deans of education would arrive to meet with the *Vocal Point* students. We were told that our visitors were looking forward to seeing how we created multimedia on the Internet.

In September, 1994, the new publications class was again a class of mixed abilities and grade levels. When these students saw what the students of the previous year had accomplished, they were excited to learn how to do the same—and challenged to even do more.

The first issue of *Vocal Point* simply contained text and two small graphics. As the students continued to explore the Internet, they discovered features which they were eager to incorporate into their newspaper. They found photos, creative uses of color, sound, and video clips! They were determined to include these features in *their* version of the *Vocal Point* in time for the Japanese visitors.

This excitement and desire to enhance *Vocal Point* to include their own ideas on multimedia was a teacher's dream. The students were driving the learning process by their utter determination and innate motivation. *Vocal Point* had truly evolved into a student-driven online publication.

THE CIRCLE OF LEARNING

In this process, students were learning from a variety of resources including paper manuals, Internet newsgroups, university students, and adults outside the school environment. This potpourri of information had to be assimilated to accomplish a given task. Once a specific job is completed, the students possess a significantly better understanding of how to do the task than anyone else. To take advantage of this process, students help future students by creating training guides for future issues of *Vocal Point*. This effort of creating teaching materials reinforces the learning process. It also perpetuates the cooperative nature of the class structure and allows for the next issue of *Vocal Point* to continue as a student-driven project.

THE PROCESS AND THE PRODUCT: A NEW PARADIGM FOR EDUCATION

The Internet is one of the most engaging new tools for K-12 students and has been highly touted for its potential impact on education. Without a context, however, random access to digital information can be an aimless, albeit educational, journey. For us, the *Vocal Point* project demonstrated the impact of this technology within the context of a specific curriculum area. For the teacher, the goals of the class are met. For the students, the journey, by their own account, has become much more real, exciting, and satisfying.

We must admit that some of the changes that we witnessed were the result of the structure of the project, and not the technology. However, the most dramatic changes did appear as a direct result of the implementation of the Internet technology. The Internet induced a change in all of the traditional classroom roles among students, teachers, and community members.

Students continued to learn from traditional research materials such as books, encyclopedias, and newspapers in the course of this project. In addition, they also used electronic sources and the opinions of a wide variety of network users. With a book, there is always an assumption that printed information is reliable. With the Internet, the students are forced to look critically at electronic resources, to verify the digital details, and only then to form their own opinions.

The perspective of students on their work is much different. Because their Internet efforts can be viewed by peers studying the same topic and by professionals in the field, students are more motivated to do a quality job. Their work is no longer just about a grade but about demonstrating to others their knowledge and skills in a given area.

The *Vocal Point* project incorporates both individual and collaborative learning. The collaborative work has expanded to include students outside of the classroom and even the school building. For example, students leaving the publications class construct guides and instructions for students in the incoming class. Students are communicating electronically with students geographically and temporally separated, in different locales and in different grade levels. This passage of experiences in digital form provides opportunities for peer education and less teacher involvement.

The structure of this project dramatically changes the "chalk-and-talk" role of the teacher. Instructors in this new environment find themselves surrendering some of the management of the learning process, which traditionally was controlled so tightly. For example, not all students need to learn about video on the Internet in a one-lecture-fits-all format. They will learn it from each other as the need arises. If all students need to learn it, the teacher can structure a process so that this happens. If it is not necessary for all students to learn how to manipulate digital video, than the real-world scenario of assuming shared responsibility in complex tasks is instilled. The students must be trusted to use this powerful technology in appropriate ways and empowered to use the technology to complete their tasks.

With the students functioning in independent roles and small groups, the role of the teacher emerged as one of facilitator, sometimes mentor, and oftentimes learner. Access to knowledgeable people and resources on the Internet provides the students with information that would not have been available in a traditional classroom. In some cases, the teacher now has opportunities to learn from the students as they applied this knowledge to the project itself.

Community members are rarely actively involved in most classrooms. The logistics of getting the right person in the right classroom at the right time is difficult. Coordination of on-going work with community members is even more complex. Electronic communication helps overcome these hurdles. With e-mail, members of the community participate on their own time and in great detail. Information arrives from community members in students' e-mail, so delays in any specific component of the project are minimal. In turn, the community plays a larger role in the project.

Additionally, the community has new opportunities to demonstrate that they care about the students and to recognize student achievement through their feedback. With *Vocal Point*, students examine big issues that will have an impact on their lives. For the students, it is significant to learn that their community cares about what they think (see Figure 2).

We believe that community involvement has been primarily responsible for the students deciding to push the project to a new level: moving from text and graphics to multimedia, and publishing a summer edition of the newspaper. In turn, these new roles in the community have empowered and motivated the students (see Figure 3).

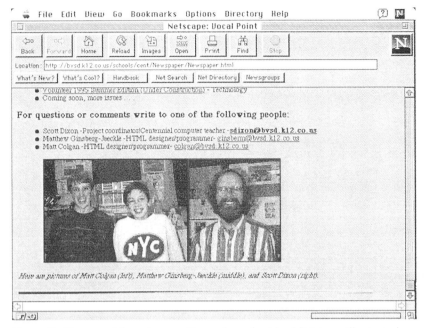

Figure 2. Two crucial student staff members for *Vocal Point* are illustrated on the home page, Matthew Ginsberg-Jaeckle and Matt Colgan. Both function as HTML programmers and taggers.

As teachers, we found it exciting to see students so motivated that on their own, they choose to extend a class project into the summer. Seeing this motivation and watching students take responsibility for their own learning is tremendously rewarding and satisfying. We look forward to the continued evolution of *Vocal Point* with the participation of international students and their diverse cultural viewpoints.

THE *VOCAL POINT* PROCESS

1. Give each student a personal Internet account. This allows them to communicate and research on their own. Extend the project beyond classroom hours. Encourage independence as well as teamwork. Include everyone in the technology. Receive feedback from the project.

2. Each student should be aware of the entire process and project and how each task is an important part of the whole picture. Identify the various roles that are needed for the project. List the background and responsibilities associated with each role. Include what learning will take place and how

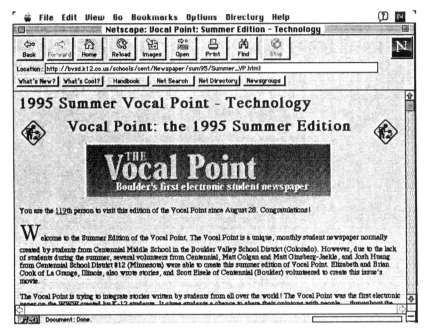

Figure 3. The summer, 1995 issue of *Vocal Point* was a joint effort of students in Colorado, Illinois, and Minnesota.

that learning will occur. Establish respect for each person's contribution and his or her assigned task. Build an appreciation for teamwork. Provide an understanding of the role of the manager. Describe how certain tasks require a different learning style from others.

3. Identify key students early. The selection of key students, to important leadership and technical roles, is important to the success of the project. Work with key students privately before identifying which students will take on which tasks. Let your students know your confidence in them and the responsibilities associated with the key tasks. Do not allow the class to vote on any issue you need to control, especially the selection of students for key tasks.

How do you select students for various roles? If you have appointed a student manager, you might allow that student to establish which students will take on the remaining roles. This gives them an immediate leadership role and helps the other students recognize the new leader. One idea is to allow the students to self-nominate for the available roles. Allow several nominations for different roles to encourage flexibility. Allow a day or so for you to consult with your student leader and individual students on their nominations. You may want to counsel some students in or out of certain tasks.

Look down the road. Do you see a "Phase Two" or second round for this project? Is it contingent on the success of phase one? Will you be able to promise students an opportunity to have the role of their choice in a future phase of the project? Remember that this is a collaborative group project, not a contest. The announcement of which students will take on which roles should not sound like an awards ceremony.

ABOUT THE AUTHORS

Scott Dixon teaches mathematics and computer science at Centennial Middle School. Along with his teaching duties, he manages the school's computer resources and sponsors Centennial's computer club. Scott's involvement in computers began during his own high school years and has continued throughout his teaching career. His Masters degree in Education focused on the integration of technology in education and he continues to strive to that end. Mail for Scott can be addressed to Centennial Middle School, 2205 Norwood Avenue, Boulder, Colorado 80304. Or phone the main office of Centennial at (303) 443–3760 or the Centennial computer lab at (303) 447–0784. E-mail for Scott can be sent to sdixon@bvsd.k12.co.us

Libby Black is the Director of the Boulder Valley Internet Project (http://bvsd.k12.co.us) and Creating Connections: Rural Teachers and the Internet. Goals of both projects include helping K-12 teachers learn how to use the Internet and develop meaningful classroom applications of the Internet. Prior to her involvement with the Boulder Valley Schools, Libby taught mathematics at the high school level. She has a BA from the College of Wooster and a Masters Degree in Secondary Mathematics Instruction and Curriculum from the Harvard Graduate School of Education. Libby's mail address is Boulder Valley School District, P. O. Box 9011, Boulder, Colorado 80301. Her phone number is (303) 447–5090 or fax to (303) 447–5024. E-mail can be sent to blackl@bvsd.k12.co.us

Interactive Internet; or, How Your School can Publish on the World Wide Web

Curtis Jensen
Area Education Agency 7
Cedar Falls, Iowa

Overview—The Numbers	
Name of School, District or State:	Area Education Agency 7 Cedar Falls, IA
Number of teachers:	4,000
Number of students:	40,000
Grades covered:	Pre-K - 12
Amount of money in grant or special expenditure (if applicable): n/a	

ABSTRACT

Internet publishing provides the means for schools to distribute information about their students, teachers, administrators, curriculum, and extracurricular activities to both local and global audiences. This chapter describes how a school can go about building a presence on the Internet including how to find an external organization to host a school's server or how to host a school's server or how to build one of your own.

BEGINNINGS

It's not enough for the staff and students of your school to surf the Internet. And it's not enough that they use the Internet as a giant library's reference collection. Nor is the Internet just a way to communicate with others far away. Your school should be an Internet publisher. How is this accomplished? This article will briefly explain that it's not difficult and not expensive. Ultimately, becoming part of the World Wide Web is a good idea for your school.

If your Internet account doesn't provide graphical access, you may think that you're not ready to be an Internet publisher. But your school has information you can share with both your immediate community and with the world. Publishing on the Web is neither incredibly difficult nor is it expensive. Web publishing brings benefits to students, staff, and your community. It is even fun!

WHY?

There are many reasons for a school to become a publisher on the Internet. One reason is to advertise your school's success and gain community support. Does your community really know what's going on in your classrooms, your buildings, or your district? How can you

Figure 1. The Cedar Rapids, Iowa, School District provides information on technology, staff, and schools on the World Wide Web.

keep them informed? Schools may not want to put a lot of resources into public relations, but it's necessary now more than ever. In Iowa, for example, a school district needs sixty percent of the participating voters to vote favorably for a bond issue in order for the measure to be approved. Yet, only about twenty percent of the eligible voters have children in the schools. Even if everyone with a child in school voted "yes" on a bond issue, there would only be a remote chance of approval. The Internet can be used as a tool to explain to the community, as a whole, the need for approval of a given bond. Research in the Cedar Falls, Iowa, community indicated that about forty percent of the homes are computer-equipped. If these computers and homes are Internet-connected, and if these households use the Internet to learn more about the schools of Cedar Falls, we assume the adults of these households will be supportive when the schools ask for additional local resources. The public benefits from the efforts of the Cedar Falls' schools in Internet publishing by learning more about education in the community. The schools, in turn, gain supporters.

Through a home page, a school can share any information provided in print such as calendars, schedules, staff directories, sports, concert, and play information, parent handbooks, and lots more. One district estimated that sixty percent of phone calls to the schools were directly related to information already announced on the radio or published in school mailings and the newspaper. School-related informa-

Figure 2. On the Ames, Iowa, High School home page, the Global Schoolhouse Project, a significant K-12 Internet resource, can be viewed.

tion seems to have a life span of less than two minutes once it arrives in a household. Even sports and parent-teacher conference schedules are lost under refrigerator magnets or paper piled on the dining room table. Publishing and maintaining school information electronically will make life easier for anyone who has to answer the question "What's for school lunch tomorrow?" twenty times a day in the administrative office (see Figures 1 and 2).

A NEW MEDIUM

Every school has artists, writers, and poets, all looking for an outlet for their efforts. Often, students put a great deal of effort into their creative projects with little hope of seeing their work on display to any audience. This student work could demonstrate to the public the value of the school as a creative environment. An Internet-based art gallery or an Internet-published collection of poetry could make a significant difference for students and the community. With the World Wide Web, there are even ways that a school can share music or movies!

How can a school move to this medium? It's not that difficult. Much printed information may already be in electronic form, on a diskette somewhere. The first step in Internet publishing is finding what already exists in digital form and collecting it. Make this step a team effort. Form a group ready to invest in this technology, with the content already stored on diskettes and hard drives. Collect this material and decide how best to organize it for the Internet.

CONNECTIONS

With electronic material in hand posting the information on an Internet server is the next step. The easiest way to publish on the Internet is to find someone with the necessary experience who's ready to help. Some universities and colleges are willing to help local schools. Look specifically for an institution with the right resources such as a dedicated Internet connection and a server. Consider approaching the college of education, the computing services unit, or even a faculty member, with connections to a local school.

Use a technique for evaluation called PNI, or Positives, Negatives, and Interesting. In any opportunity, look for the Positives and Negatives in each choice, as well as those aspects that are just plain Interesting. In Internet publishing with a university, the positive aspects of the decision are the rich experiences academic institutions have with

Internet resources. For a university, information about a local school won't use much disk space or computing time. On the negative side, a school depending on a college or university will always rely on someone outside to make the project work. There are other priorities for the university, and so they will be less committed to the task. On the interesting angle, contacts made by the school to the university eventually could lead to productive future projects for both parties.

Alternatively, Free-Nets are an excellent possibility. Free-Nets are local information providers that usually make community resources available electronically. Free-Nets are usually very interested in involving schools in their networks.

In Iowa, one Free-Net CedarNet, is dedicated to making local information available to a wide audience (see Figure 3). Those without computers at home use CedarNet at public access sites such as libraries, schools, and a few local businesses. On the plus side, Free-Nets are experienced at making information available to the public. On the minus side, again someone else will control ultimately information about the school. Free-Nets have the distinct advantage of being a lot like public libraries with no charges to users of the service.

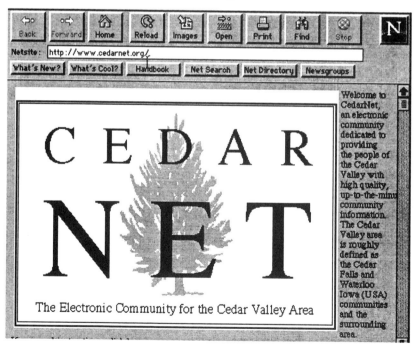

Figure 3. The home page for CedarNet provides details on Waterloo and the Cedar Valley area in northeast Iowa.

No university, no Free-Net? Then propose Internet connectivity and publication for a school to a local commercial organization. Start with those in the company with connections to the school and make a case for support of the publishing project. For the corporation, their sponsorship is excellent public relations and really will not cost them very much in terms of time and resources. Pluses? School-business partnerships create fascinating opportunities for both corporations and education.

Still searching? There are companies that, for a fee, will provide space on a server and Internet expertise. On the plus side of this sort of arrangement, a school will enter into a well-defined contract with an organization with clearly defined responsibilities for all parties. The cost for such an approach is not as great as independently securing an Internet connection, securing necessary hardware and software, loading the data, and maintaining the site.

REQUIREMENTS

If a school decides to become its own Internet publisher, it will require access to the Internet, hardware and software, and Internet-savvy information. Look on the Internet for Web 66, a site dedicated to K-12 Internet solutions, for answers on how other schools have solved this problem (see Figure 4).

The first step is locating an Internet service provider. A provider purchases a large "pipeline" to the Internet and resells smaller "pipes" or connections to others. Shop around and compare prices. Inexperienced or poorly operated providers may provide inexpensive service, but at a huge cost in terms of time and support. A provider should connect all networked computers in a school to the Internet without the need for a modem and phone line for every computer. A direct connection to the Internet is a very powerful tool and will probably involve not only the Internet provider but the local telephone company as well.

Internet hardware and software will also be needed, such as a router and a server. The router, for example, allows the school network to physically connect to the Internet. Finding and purchasing this equipment is usually a shared decision with the Internet provider. The provider will require specific equipment that they support, so involve the provider in these acquisitions. The provider should also register the school formally with InterNIC, the organization that formally records Internet sites. Internet names for schools usually take the form

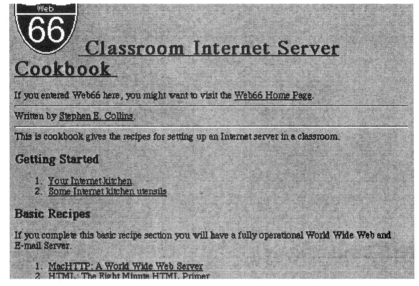

Figure 4. Web 66 gives educators and students the basics on becoming an Internet publisher.

of domain-name.K12.state.country For example, at Area Education Agency 7, the District is known as aea7.K12.ia.us

SERVERS

A server is also necessary. This is a computer to provide school information on the Internet and the World Wide Web. Being a part of the Internet once meant that you had to learn UNIX. Fortunately for schools now, there are ways to be part of the Internet using Apple Macintoshes or Intel-based computers as servers.

Some 25 per cent of the Internet servers today are Macintoshes. With a program called MacHTTP, Macintosh users can turn their computers into Internet servers. MacHTTP is available from StarNine Technologies (http://www.biap.com/machttp/machttp_software.html). Apple Computer has put together a Macintosh Internet server with much Internet software already loaded on its hard disk. Information about it can be found at http://www.solutions.apple.com/internet/default.html

With an Internet server, information will need to be formatted for the World Wide Web. That will require training in the HyperText Markup Language or HTML. HTML is a markup, not a programming, language. Its successful application, however, requires some thought and time. There are plenty of books about HTML and much information about HTML on the Internet. To make a school home page look professional, add graphics and work on a well-designed overall appearance. If possible, include someone with experience in computer graphics on the school publishing team.

CONCLUSION

When your Web page is up and running, you'll have made progress towards meeting your responsibility to be more than a consumer on the Internet. You will have improved your school's public relations program and helped your community learn more about its schools.

Don't let your Web publishing program end with your first effort. Keep your school's home page a dynamic document, changing and growing just like your students and your district. Good luck, and I look forward to seeing the address of your home page posted soon on the Internet.

ABOUT THE AUTHOR

Curtis Jensen is the Administrator for Production and Technology Support Services at the Area Education Agency 7 in Cedar Falls, Iowa. He spent eleven years as a classroom teacher followed by eleven years as a school library media specialist. Curt is on the Board of Directors of CedarNet, a Community Free-Net in the Cedar River Valley of northeast Iowa (http://www.CedarNet.org). Mail will find Curt at the Area Education Agency 7, 3712 Cedar Heights Drive, Cedar Falls, IA 50613. Voice messages to (319) 273–8241 or fax to (319) 273–8243. Electronic mail can be sent to cjensen@cedarnet.org

Constructing Educational Web Pages: Moving Beyond "Show and Tell"

Caroline McCullen
Teacher
Ligon GT Magnet Middle School
Raleigh, North Carolina

Overview—The Numbers	
Name of School, District or State:	Ligon GT Magnet Middle School Wake County Public Schools Raleigh, NC
Number of teachers:	65
Number of students:	1,200
Grades covered:	6-8
Amount of money in grant or special expenditure (if applicable): none allocated for this project	

ABSTRACT

What makes a successful home page? Why are some educational sites on the Internet accessed more than others? Creating useful and entertaining home pages on the Internet depends on several key components, including relevant content, the right mix of text and graphics, and helpful pointers to other sites. This chapter discusses several key aspects for creating interesting web pages for your school.

GET ON THE NET!

In the first six months of 1995, World Wide Web (WWW) travelers witnessed a tremendous scramble as K-12 schools increased their presence in cyberspace. The goal of many educators was to develop a presence on the WWW in the form of a home page. Opportunities for schools were abundant as several commercial organizations were hosting home pages for schools without the necessary technical and financial resources.

Why did some of these educational sites generate a great deal of traffic, while others were hardly used? Why were a favored few chosen for hot lists all over the Internet, while others were visited only by their authors and a few friends? The answers can be found in the choice of content and the actual design of the pages. When teachers undertake the time-consuming, labor-intensive chore of constructing their own pages in the HyperText Markup Language (HTML), a little careful planning before any tagging begins will make a great deal of difference in the final product.

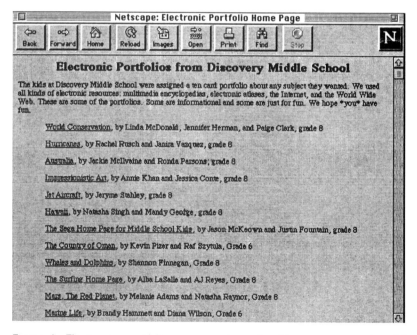

Figure 1. Electronic portfolios on a variety of subjects were produced by students at Discovery Middle School in Orlando, Florida and posted on the World Wide Web.

RELEVANT CONTENT

Let's look at a few of the options for content within a home page. For example, digital cameras, such as Apple's QuickTake, provide an opportunity to post images of students on the Internet. Although students enjoy seeing their images and biographies on their own personal pages, rarely will a student explore more than one or two of these electronic calling cards. If our goal is to find readers of the contents of our pages, contents that emphasize the academic work of students and not their personalities, then building biographical home pages with digital images is not a wise approach.

Indeed, security has to be a very real concern when posting personal information about students. It is comparable to posting personal information on a bulletin board in a busy airport or shopping mall. Would we encourage our students to do that? Hardly! Consequently, we must resist the temptation to post pictures and personal facts, even if it is exciting to see images of ourselves in cyberspace. Alternatives exist where images can be printed and mailed or the File Transfer Protocol (FTP) can be used to transmit images electronically to keypals of students in other schools.

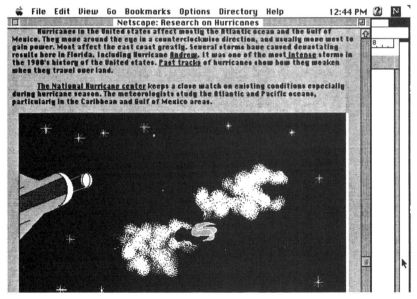

Figure 2. A specific student portfolio examines hurricanes and includes a pointer to the National Hurricane Center. This site was found by using search tools on the Internet to locate information about hurricanes and violent storms.

A more content-rich home page will contain actual work, in text, graphics, and other formats, completed by the students. For example, research projects, book and software reviews, and original art are excellent ways to use this medium (see Figure 1). Nevertheless, we have to strive to go beyond simply constructing a "show and tell" page of our students' best work (see Figure 2).

COLLABORATION IS THE KEY

One way in which home pages can be made more interesting is by including data generated by a wide variety of participants. A display of book reports written by one classroom might interest a few readers. A collection of book reports from several schools around the world would probably interest many readers for a wide range of reasons. Social studies teachers might compare the variety of cultures reflected in the reports. English teachers might use the variety of reports to stimulate a discussion of literature in different countries. Individual readers might compare their own impressions of certain

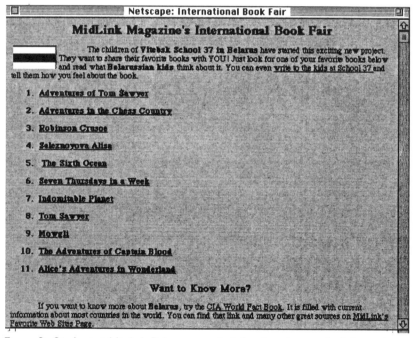

Figure 3. Students in Vitebsk, Belarus post their book reviews and ask for reviews by other students in *MidLink Magazine*'s International Book Fair (http://longwood.cs.ucf.edu/~MidLink).

books to those of distant peers reflected in the posted reports. In the student-generated *MidLink Magazine* (http://longwood.cs.ucf.edu/ ~MidLink), students in Vitebsk, Belarus compare book reviews with fellow students from all over the world. This International Book Fair in *MidLink Magazine* provides a substantial resource to the global Internet audience (see Figure 3).

Collaboration can also involve schools and business partners. Explor-A-Link is a cooperative project involving the Enloe Magnet High School, Ligon GT Magnet Middle School, BellSouth Business Systems, and the Children's Museum in Raleigh, North Carolina. These agencies cooperate to create real exhibits in the actual museum, as well as digital exhibits for a virtual museum under construction. In this effort, students collect data, send e-mail, and collaborate with others in the global Internet community to construct the exhibits.

THE PAGE YOU CALL "HOME"

How can you develop your own home page? Begin by asking a few questions. What do we have in common with our global neighbors? What is a common occurrence, geographical feature, or social custom that we might experience in different ways? What could we compare or contrast with others? What will students truly find interesting in another culture? After brainstorming with colleagues using e-mail, most teachers can find a few ideas that fit into what they are already doing in their classrooms.

GUIDELINES FOR SUCCESS

Here are a few guidelines that will help as you design your own home page.

First, keep it simple! Even what seems like the simplest project in the beginning can easily become too complex to finish. Pick only one element or feature that you would like to compare or contrast. Resist the temptation to include related data in your project results; ultimately they will distract your readers rather than enhance your project. A sound project requires only one or two components from each participant.

Second, look first at what you are already doing in your school. What information could you gather that would enhance your curriculum? Avoid inventing something completely new and out of context. Instead, try a new slant on some project that you've already completed.

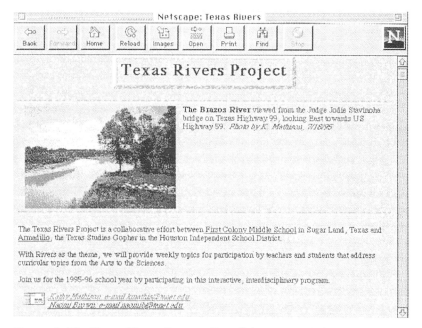

Figure 4. The Texas Rivers Project (http://chico.rice.edu/armadillo/Ftbend/ rivers.html) incorporates interdisciplinary lesson plans and invites other students to collect and compare data about their rivers on the Internet.

For example, if in social studies you've already tackled the major rivers of the world, why not gather data about other rivers from Internet-connected colleagues? For example, Kathy Jo Mathison at First Colony Middle School in Sugarland, Texas, developed a project about rivers directly from her social studies curriculum (see Figure 4). In her Texas Rivers project, she put objectives, procedures, graphics, and assignments on her home page. After her students posted some of their work, she invited other states to join them. The excellent results can be viewed at http://chico.rice.edu/armadillo/Ftbend/rivers.html

Third, decide exactly what you will require of all participants in the project. Will they send you the results by e-mail? If so, make up a template that includes every piece of information that you'll require of them. Don't forget their names, locations, schools, grades, and electronic addresses. I have often received data from some unknown Internet surfer who submits his information and then becomes mysteriously "lost in cyberspace."

Some of the most interesting partners are likely to have limited resources. It is to your benefit to make it as easy as possible for them to participate, even if they can only send you e-mail. You can add their information to your own page with a minimum of labor. If they can't submit everything properly tagged or even digitized, a little extra typing on your part can create a unique resource.

Fourth, set a firm timeline and publish it along with your original announcement. When is your project closed to participants? Or will it remain open? When is everything due in your mailbox? If you intend to post your results on the Web, remember that you can easily update your page to include late returns. For example, a deadline is absolutely crucial if you are tabulating results since percentages can change a great deal if just one or two sites are left out of the sample.

Fifth, take advantage of the medium. Use e-mail to stay in touch with your participants. Make sure they are working on assignments and project plans. They may need encouragement or help from you but may be reluctant to ask. A friendly posting during the project can prevent disappointment later.

Sixth, decide what you will do with the results. Will you gather all results and post them? Will each site tabulate and post their own? If participants have the means to post their own work, the simplest method should be to include links on your page actually pointing to their servers and sites. Distributing a template in HTML to all participants will make the project acquire an even flow, feel, and tone. In it there can be "Back to the Home Page" or "Back to the _____ Project" links.

Finally, consider how long it takes for those with the most basic kind of Internet connection to view your graphics. Keep images simple and small. Locate large files well within imbedded links. Loading twenty graphics onto one page condemns you automatically to just a few visitors. As always, quality is far more important than quantity because long loading times for a large batch of graphics can discourage even the most determined Internet user. Students are especially notorious for abandoning even the most excellent sites because of an abundance of large graphic files.

CALL FOR PARTICIPATION

Once you have a sound idea for an Internet project and home page, find partners. One way to locate participants is to post an announcement on an active LISTSERV. Kidsphere is one of the oldest and best LISTSERVs designed just for teachers. Many Kidsphere readers and subscribers are helpful to beginners (see Figure 5). Even experienced Internet users continue to subscribe to Kidsphere because of the

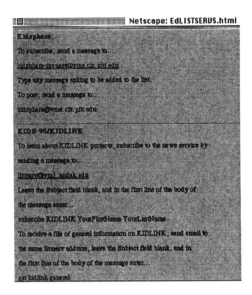

Figure 5. Information about many K-12 LISTSERVs can be found at http://
www.asd.k12.ak.us/EdLISTSERVS.html

freshness of ideas posted on it, the general tone of the list, and the
high level of activity. To subscribe to Kidsphere, send a message to
kidsphere-request@vms.cis.pitt.edu

Once subscribed, read messages posted to the list to understand
the interests of those subscribed. Once you are familiar with the list's
culture, begin to compose your project announcement for posting.
Your initial post to the LISTSERV is extremely important. Be sure to
include a signature file that will contain your name, school, location,
and electronic address. Keep in mind that your message may be cop-
ied and posted on other lists. A spelling error, a miscalculation of dates
or times, or the omission of some crucial information may come back
to haunt you and seriously hinder your project. Have a friend examine your announcement before posting. Then have another colleague
proofread it one last time before you finally click on the "Send" but-
ton.

RESPONDING

Now your work begins in earnest. As you receive inquiries from interested parties as a result of your posting, answer their questions
promptly. Be sure to attach your signature file to every message you
send. Keep copies of all correspondence. Even with a few participants,

it is easy to forget what you said in your last message. If you seem confused or often repeat yourself, your potential participants will lose interest.

Try to seek partners from distant regions to form a core group, since they will probably provide the most interesting information to your students. Once you get a group of teachers to commit to the project, begin by constructing a preliminary home page for the project. Post this draft home page and ask those with Web access to provide you with feedback about it. Take advantage of the Web as a proverbial global conference room and use it to construct a page that will appeal to your entire group.

If you are just learning HTML, take advantage of interactive resources on the Internet. For example, use the Beginner's Guide to HTML, which can be found at the National Center for Supercomputing Applications (NCSA) of the University of Illinois at http://www.ncsa.uiuc.edu/demoweb/html-primer.html This guide describes how to construct many aspects of a home page with basic elements of HTML (see Figure 6).

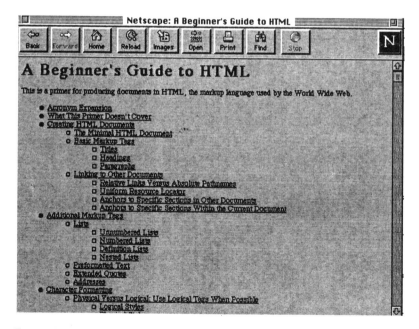

Figure 6. The interactive pages of the Beginner's Guide to HTML provide excellent tutorials for those just starting to use HTML (http://www.ncsa.uiuc.edu/demoweb/html-primer.html).

An excellent LISTSERV for those working on Internet educational projects is WWWEdu (pronounced "We Do"), or the World Wide Web in Education. This LISTSERV, maintained by Andy Carvin, is one of the largest and most active lists devoted to the WWW. It is an excellent place to find answers to technical or philosophical questions regarding the Web in the classroom. To subscribe, send a message to listproc@kudzu.cnidr.org and in the body of the message write "subscribe wwwedu (your name)"

INVITE THE WORLD!

Once you've designed and constructed your page, check every link to ensure that they work properly before publicly announcing your project. Visitors greeted with the "File Not Found" error message may never return. Once you've checked your links, invite the world to your server and home page. Write a concise, but enticing, announcement about your project. Tell readers and visitors that you will be happy to share your results. Teachers are more likely to participate in a project if they know what benefits they will receive in exchange for their time. If you intend for your project to be ongoing, make it easy for those viewing your page to join your project. Include an electronic form or template on which they can submit their data online.

CONCLUSION

We are entering the a time when teachers are bringing entire classes online with Internet-connected computers. Already, some teachers are placing lessons for the week on a home page and asking students to complete and turn their assignments in electronically. Students and educators will select their digital destinations with the same criteria used to evaluate traditional, published materials: content, format, and ease of use. Internet publishers remembering these basic factors will meet with success. Creating viable resources ultimately enables teachers to take advantage of the full collaborative potential of the Internet.

ABOUT THE AUTHOR

Caroline McCullen teaches telecommunications classes at Ligon GT Magnet Middle School in Raleigh, North Carolina. A recipient of a Disney Teacheriffic Award in 1994, she serves on the Advisory Board of the Assembly for Computers in English. Her articles about telecommunications in the classroom have been included in the *Florida English Journal, The Writing Notebook, The Florida Technology in Education Quarterly*, and the ISTE's Learning and Leading with Technology. Her students publish the collaborative digital magazine known as *MidLink Magazine* which can be found at http://longwood.cs.ucf.edu/~MidLink. She may be contacted at caroline_mccullen@ncsu.edu or phone (919) 856–7929 or fax (919) 856–3745.

Imagine the Possibilities: Exploring the Internet with Middle School Students

Barbara Spitz
Integration Specialist
Instructional Technologies
Madison Metropolitan School District
Madison, Wisconsin

Overview—The Numbers	
Name of School, District or State:	Madison Middle School Madison Metropolitan School District Madison, WI
Number of teachers:	30
Number of students:	240
Grades covered:	6-8
Amount of money in grant or special expenditure (if applicable): n/a	

ABSTRACT

Internet access at Madison Middle School 2000 brought new opportunities and challenges for teaching and learning. The past two years of Internet access in the school has emphasized the need for and benefits of partnerships with the community. Specific successful projects have included posting information about the school on the Internet; promoting the community with a Web page; and publishing student research on the school's server.

GETTING STARTED

In the spring of 1993, an experimental school of choice, focusing on an integrated curriculum, technology, and a multicultural perspective, became a reality in Madison, Wisconsin. Supported by the Madison Metropolitan School District, it is called Madison Middle School 2000 (MMS 2000). I was asked to be the technology resource instructor for the school.

DESIGNING THE NETWORK

The announcement of a new middle school, and its technology focus, sparked the interest of Professor Larry Landweber of the University of Wisconsin (UW) Computer Science Department. In the summer of 1993, he initiated a process that would provide the school with Internet access. Cisco Systems, a California-based company which builds Internet tools, offered the school a router to assist their connection to the Internet.

Professor Landweber, Principal Offie Hobbs, and I pulled together a team to plan and implement technology in the school. This group included Paul Beebe and Jay Rosenbloom from the UW–Madison Computer Science Department and Division of Information Technology (DoIT); knowledgeable parents of enrolled students; and hardware system engineers. After much discussion, the team developed a connectivity plan which included a Technology Learning Center (TLC). It accommodates an entire classroom, with five computers in each classroom. There are eight computers in the Library Media Center (LMC), a CD-ROM tower on the file server, and Internet access via an ISDN line to the University. There are also peripherals such as printers, scanners, VCRs, video laser disc players, digital cameras, video cameras, televisions, an LCD panel, and other equipment. All computers are networked and connected to the Internet.

PROVIDING TECHNICAL ASSISTANCE

Thanks to the design team, everything worked! Professor Landweber rounded up volunteer graduate students whom we could call upon for help. In addition, we hired a technician, Tara Vraniak, for technical support (see Figure 1). For those of us who had struggled for years to obtain technology, support was crucial in keeping all of the equipment operational.

Figure 1. School technician Tara Vraniak is with the first group of students to become certified in computer maintenance.

INTEGRATING THE INTERNET INTO THE CURRICULUM

Since the school focused on student-centered, integrated, and thematic curricula, few textbooks were purchased. We explored the Internet as a way for students to connect to up-to-date resources from around the world. The Internet also provided the means for students and staff to communicate with faraway places and to share investigations and research with others.

We started with a special interest group called "Exploring the Internet" for sixth grade students (see Figure 2). In this group, students created a booklet that would explore the Internet with Gopher. It included a brief description of the development of the Internet, responsible use of it, resources on the Internet, and a student-generated Internet Hunt. The booklet was used by teachers, students, and parents. Bookmarks to useful Gopher servers were linked to an icon in At Ease, our front-end network security program. This process worked quite well during the 1993-94 school year.

We also took advantage of developments in Internet tools. For example, we started using the Internet searching software, Apple-Search, in the fall of 1994. It provided a new vehicle for students to search the Internet, allowing access to some 500 educationally-oriented and text-based Wide Area Information Servers (WAIS).

Figure 2. A Madison Middle School 2000 student explores the Internet with an adult guest.

CREATING A WORLD WIDE WEB HOME PAGE

Late in 1994, we acquired Netscape software and began our exploring the World Wide Web (WWW). Students found Netscape's multimedia capabilities of text, graphics, sound, video, and animation appealing (see Figure 3). A special interest group of sixth graders reviewed many sites on the Web in order to create links to useful electronic resources. Favorite sites included a dinosaur exhibit in Hawaii, the Exploratorium in San Francisco, the Louvre in Paris, and the White House in Washington, D. C.

Within a few weeks of this activity, students were asking about putting together a home page for the school. Being total novices at the HyperText Markup Language (HTML), we turned to a volunteer UW Computer Science graduate student, Michael Lee, for assistance. Michael helped us find instructions on turning our file server in the school into a Web server (http://198.150.8.9). We explored HTML, and decided that our first attempt at a home page would contain links to our favorite resources. We added information about the school and scanned in a graphic of our school mascot, created by one of the sixth graders.

PROMOTING MADISON ON THE WEB

I asked my sixth grade students what we could do with the school home page (see Figure 4). One student's suggestion, to include electronic information about Madison, drew almost unanimous enthusiasm. "Life in Madison" became the theme of the next special interest group. Students generated a list of topics about Madison and then categorized the list into topics such as "places to visit" and "special events." Students then investigated the categories with teams of students working on specific subjects.

We approached the Madison Chamber of Commerce and Madison Convention and Visitors Bureau for brochures and information. They were so pleased with the idea of students promoting Madison on the Internet that they volunteered to work with us. Students also acquired information via letters, phone calls, interviews, and surveys.

Figure 3. Professor Larry Landweber of the Computer Science Department at the University of Wisconsin works with a MMS 2000 student.

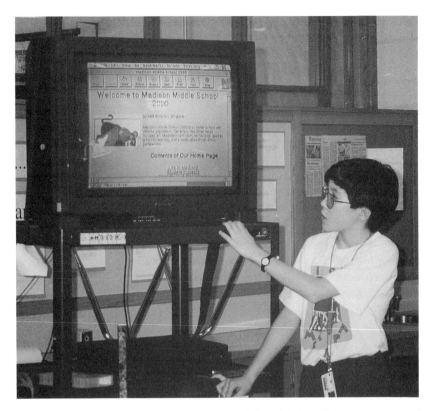

Figure 4. A MMS 2000 student explains the "Life in Madison" project to several guests of the school.

Students took photos, scanned them, and imported them into the home page. The project continued until the end of the school year, by which time, all sixth graders had contributed to the project.

PUBLISHING STUDENT PROJECTS ON THE INTERNET

In the spring of 1995, I decided to publish student-authored reports on the school home page. What kind of reports? For example, students in one class had worked hard on their research on health issues. With permission of the students, their reports appeared on the Internet, with the potential of a very large readership (see Figure 5).

It did not take long to find out if these papers were useful. A sixth grader's report on acupuncture was accessed by a doctor at the University of Virginia Medical School. The doctor responded by e-mail that he was so impressed with the report that he made a link to it

Figure 5. Superintendent Cheryl Wilhoyte is taken on a tour of the Internet with a MMS 2000 student.

from his "Complimentary Medicine" home page. An educator in San Diego was "amazed" at a report on steroids by another sixth grader. A Coordinator of Instructional Technologies in Arizona remarked that a paper by a seventh grader, on a community service project with a nursing home, was extraordinary. This recognition reinforced the students' self-esteem. It created a model for setting high expectations, taking responsibility for one's own work, and striving for excellence.

Our server was experiencing a great deal of traffic, as well. Within the first four months of the posting of the school home page, the server was visited over 40,000 times from sites in over forty countries. A student report on prostate cancer was accessed 107 times in the month of May. Reading the server log indeed was exciting and interesting!

PUBLIC RELATIONS: INVITING THE GOVERNOR

In spring, 1994, the state legislature was deliberating the Wisconsin Information Superhighway Bill. We invited the Governor and legislators to the school to learn how students were using the Internet in the classroom (see Figure 6). Governor Tommy Thompson and some thirty legislators accepted the invitation. It was a wonderful way to

Figure 6. The Governor and state legislators attend a "Teach In" at the school on the Internet.

share the potential of the Internet in education with those making decisions about support. It also promoted the school and its educational opportunities to a wide and diverse audience. The Governor promised the students on his visit that if the bill passed through the Legislature, he would actually sign it into law at the school. It passed and on July 5, 1994, the Governor returned to sign the bill in our school.

MORE PUBLIC RELATIONS: PARTICIPATING IN A PBS SPECIAL

The North Central Regional Education Laboratory (NCREL) was looking for schools to include in a PBS Special titled "Merging Onto the Information Super Highway." Since the school was currently using the Internet, it provided an excellent example of classroom applications of networking. Filming took place in September, 1994. When the Special was aired in December, 1994, we were amazed that our use of the Internet had changed in just a few months. For example, during the filming students were using Gopher and AppleSearch. By December, we had moved to the Web browser Netscape and had already created our own school home page.

PRESENTING TO COMMUNITY LEADERS

We decided to share our Internet classroom stories locally (see Figure 7). We invited Mayor Paul Soglin and the Superintendent of Madison Schools, Cheryl Wilhoyte, to learn about the "Life in Madison" project. On other occasions, we invited parents to school in order to show them how students were using the Internet. We also described our Internet experiences at a state middle school conference and a state librarian conference.

These presentations led to more interest in the Internet activities of the school. The media felt that the stories were newsworthy so features appeared in newspapers and on news broadcasts. Our own educational channel broadcast some classroom events and interest in our classroom Internet experiences brought many visitors to our school. In spring, 1995, MMS 2000 was selected as a national award winner of Community Solutions in Education, sponsored by several national businesses and initiated by the Education Department of the newspaper "USA Today."

Figure 7. Madison Mayor Paul Soglin meets with community leaders and students to learn more about the "Life in Madison" project.

REFLECTING ON OUR EXPERIENCES

The integration of the Internet into the Madison Middle School 2000 has been an exciting adventure. It has provided me with the best teaching and learning experiences of my career. My colleagues in this exploration have been and will continue to be my students. Together we are trying to figure out how to find our way around the Internet by learning from each other.

Most of my teaching colleagues will agree that integration of the Internet has changed the teacher's role. They realize that they are no longer the sole information provider, but rather they are more effective as a facilitator, mentor, or co-explorer. I believe that all students have a natural curiosity and a desire to know and understand. More learning will take place when teachers focus on supporting students in creating their own work.

The introduction of the Internet has brought varying responses from teachers. Some long time teachers have had difficulty changing their role in the classroom and prefer to continue their old teaching habits. At the other end of the spectrum, some teachers feel that limiting access to the Internet for students is censorship and violates personal freedom. Most teachers fall somewhere in between those two extremes.

There are vast amounts of information on the Internet for students. Students need help in learning what to do with this information beyond merely accessing it. Access to information does not equal knowledge. Our job, as educators, is to help students use information to create their own personal knowledge by linking new information to what they already know.

Access to the Internet can promote equity in education. It can level the playing field by providing equal access to information. I also see the Internet as the vehicle that will bring all institutions in the community together in a meaningful and purposeful way. When students feel that their work is valued, meaningful, and useful to others, they will be motivated to become participating and contributing citizens in their community.

ABOUT THE AUTHOR

Barbara Spitz is presently an Integration Specialist in the Instructional Technologies Department of the Madison Metropolitan School District. She received her Ph.D. from the University of Wisconsin at Madison in 1994. For the past decade, she has explored new ways to teach and to learn in an effort to assist diverse populations in education. Her main interests have been in integrating the curriculum and incorporating technology into the curriculum as a tool for education. Mail will reach her at 545 West Dayton Street, Madison, WI 53703, phone (608) 266–6007, fax (608) 266–6275, e-mail to bspitz@madison.k12.wi.us. Barbara's home page for the MMSD Instructional Technologies Department can be found at http://danenet.wicip.org/mmsd-it/

Part V:

Postscript

Postscript
Learning with the Internet: Prospects for Tomorrow

Kim Rose
Apple Computer, Inc.
Learning Concepts Group

ABSTRACT

Schools and libraries have begun a brave and pioneering effort to explore how to use the Internet in their communities. Leaders in this effort have discovered that Internet access holds the promise of amplifying learning and altering learning environments. This medium can also act as a vehicle to assist students in understanding complex issues. The Internet, and specifically the World Wide Web, can be used more effectively in learning by changing teaching methodologies and philosophies.

INTRODUCTION

The men and women who have shared their projects in this book are to be commended for their efforts. They have certainly been on the bleeding edge of this new medium by exploring its potential in their educational institutions and classrooms.

It has been no easy task for any of us to put networks in place in our schools and libraries. Few really understand the time and dedication it takes to build an infrastructure of both equipment and people to support the Internet in a learning center. In most cases, those who put these networks in place are by no means computer and telecommunications networking specialists. These teachers and librarians have learned an entirely new vocabulary and completely new processes to make their networks a reality.

In the course of this process, educators, administrators, librarians, and researchers have formed new alliances with government agencies, community organizations, and businesses such as local telephone companies and hardware vendors. Some of these pioneers who are now using networked information in their daily lives struggled along without even a single telephone in their classroom not too long ago.

What has been done to date is to create an infrastructure comprised of hardware, software, and a human support system. Now comes the hardest work: dealing with the content, the information for which this entire structure was created. The real challenge remains.

What comes after children have searched for facts in Internet treasure hunts? What will happen after they've exchanged e-mail with their peers in other cities and countries? What follows after students have published their own home pages on the World Wide Web? Is there something better than searching for world facts or eye-catching graphics?

The development of meaningful content, and the creation of a curriculum which weaves the use of the Internet into it, are the real challenges for tomorrow. We need to teach life's metaskills. We need to teach young people how to be ready to question, to explore, and to argue with each other in meaningful ways. We need to teach different modes of thinking and different ways to use the imagination. How can we use the Internet achieve these goals?

Let me take an example from my work with several schools in the Los Angeles area. Recently, a fourth and fifth grade class constructed periscopes as part of their science curriculum. After making periscopes out of PVC tubing with two mirrors placed at forty-five degree angles, students were asked to go to the playground and use the periscopes to explore the world around them. They were then asked to record their observations, thoughts, and questions.

After some experimentation, children wrote comments like, "the library was upside down, the street was right side up, the bus was upside down, the ground was on the sky." Not one child questioned this phenomenon, but readily accepted this crazy change to their world and wrote it down. Additionally, none of the children were intrigued with how the periscope accomplished its illusions. How can we blame them? In this modern world, these changes may seem trivial.

It is tragic that many children readily accept the world around them with a credulity that is similar to that of those who lived in the Middle Ages. A mission of our educational system must be to revitalize our children's imaginations. It is critical that we teach our children how to think abstractly and in a nonlinear fashion.

RUSHING ONTO THE SUPERHIGHWAY

The Information Superhighway, the Web, Gopher, telnet, FTP, networking—these are the latest buzzwords used today in schools throughout the world. We have to be careful that these technological fixes are not the next band-aid for education. Computers, software, networks, and cables in our schools will not change the way our children think. We need to use these technologies in new ways to take advantage of the possibilities that the medium offers. Pessimistically, these new technologies may be used in ways which just mimic the old and not gain us any new insights into creating better learning environments.

Technology is employed in classrooms today in two ways: "telling technology" and "doing technology." A group of students passively viewing a lecture transmitted by cable on the destruction of the rain forest is an example of "telling technology." "Doing technology" employs the same students studying the same phenomena, but actively engages them in acquiring data, comparing opinions, and exchanging information with fellow learners and experts around the globe. And yes, for a break, they watch the video downlink.

Students become fully empowered when technology is employed as "doing technology." In this mode, they have an opportunity to turn information into knowledge and develop a true understanding of complex material. The Internet holds promise as a wonderful vehicle to promote such learning.

RETHINKING DISTANCE LEARNING

To many, distance learning means arranging for a specialist to deliver a lecture to a group of students in a remote area. By doing this, we are turning computer monitors into television sets. Perhaps we are not even using computer monitors at all, but using telephone lines or satellite technology to deliver television to our classrooms. We need to think beyond the medium that we have been passively watching for the past four decades. We need to create a new vocabulary with new definitions to exploit our new media fully.

The challenge lies in creating virtual learning environments where students can come together via networks to engage in collaborative learning situations. Today some schools use the Internet merely to facilitate electronic correspondence courses. What kinds of interfaces and tools can we design to exploit this medium, to change these correspondence courses into creative exchanges?

WHAT IS COMPUTER LITERACY?

Computer literacy is *not* learning the location of the on and off switch on a CPU or even knowing what CPU means. Like literacy in other domains, to be computer literate you must be able to recreate ideas from representations—reading—and from that material you must be able to construct representations of complex ideas—writing. Students need to become facile manipulators of information to the extent that they can find it, think about what they have found, sort through various points of view, and then form their own opinions. They need to go beyond reading essays to creating their own. The act of generating ideas and arguments needs to span all disciplines—language, mathematics, the arts, and sciences. We are just beginning to explore the potential in which computers and networks can transform our children into fully literate adults.

The Internet can be a wonderful tool for learners to become more literate. We must be careful not to confuse information gathering with growth in knowledge. Sending children on Internet scavenger hunts may prove useful in honing their skills with Internet tools, but it doesn't create knowledge.

Navigating the Internet nevertheless requires an important kind of thinking on the part of the user and it should not be overlooked. When challenged to find information on a particular topic, a student can choose several directions and has many tools available to assist that choice. Students will often have to shift their thinking in order to find the appropriate material.

I am working with one group of students that is using the Internet as a resource to find information on whales. Each student is studying a different type of whale such as the fin whale, narwhal, or killer whale. I observed one child as she searched for information on her whale's breeding habits. In her first query she entered the words "killer whale." This approach did not provide her with very much. Upon further thought, she said, "The scientific name for the killer whale is 'Orca.' Let's search under that." Using this refined search, she found some valuable information.

Computer literacy in the future will include an ability to use tools designed for total manipulation of the media. In other words, children who are computer literate will be able to not only use prepackaged software applications but will also be facile in using telecommunications tools. They will obtain information and exchange ideas on computer networks. They will write their own programs to broaden their persuasive writing in local and wider virtual learning environments.

WHAT IS MEANINGFUL LEARNING?

How can teachers provide a meaningful learning environment? Children need to learn to approach problems in various ways so they can later think about the information they find, digest it, and formulate their own opinions. They need to develop their intuitions about the world. Learners need to be encouraged to use combinations of whatever resources are available to them. When challenged with a project, our children should be encouraged to access information from books, magazines, CD-ROMs, and other people, in person, with e-mail or by the telephone. Children should think first about what combination of resources they might use to assist them. Using resources in this way will create a meaningful learning environment, one where the student is at the center of their learning and will be learning for understanding.

Teaching methodologies also must change with new media. Teachers must assume the role as co-learner and facilitator with their students. We have read about some wonderful examples of this shift in teaching in chapters of this book. Indeed, the rapid development of technology has made it more difficult for teachers to keep ahead of their students. This information explosion demands change, but it is a difficult change for many teachers.

To no longer be positioned as the central source for all facts, but to step down from that role and say to the student "let's find out together" takes a lot of courage. We will only create more powerful learning situations for our children if teachers are willing to adopt this courageous attitude. Many teachers are coming forward and engaging themselves with their students in new environments such as the World Wide Web.

THE WORLD WIDE WEB

I'd like to explore the idea of utilizing the World Wide Web as a new and valuable medium. It is another "place to go" for learning and one which can be used in conjunction with people, places, books, and the telephone. Because of its dynamic makeup, the Web can be a fantastic tool for constructivist learning. It can be used as a means to gain understanding into complex systems and ideas.

To be used in a meaningful way, we need to embed this medium into a context. Teachers must guide its use and provide direction to set the stage for deep learning, not merely using it to gather disjointed information.

First, the Web can be seen as a source for reference material. It houses an abundance of basic reference sources, including the Encyclopaedia Britannica or EB Online. Resources like EB Online are taking advantage of the medium, with links between encyclopedia entries and other Internet resources. The Web also serves as a virtual library of libraries. Learners can now gather information from public and private libraries around the world.

The Web can amplify a learning experience or broaden a student's insight into a subject area study. Fourth and fifth graders studying World War II and the Holocaust can now take a virtual trip through the Holocaust Museum in Washington, D. C. Science activities can be amplified by virtually visiting science centers such as San Francisco's Exploratorium or Canada's Ontario Science Center. The Web can provide the basis for collaborative and comparative learning.

Perhaps one of the most exciting uses of the Internet and World Wide Web is its potential to connect people. There is always a "who" behind the "what" you discover on the Web and often e-mail addresses are available to make the connections. A curious reader can get more information by directly sending mail to a site's Webmaster or those persons listed as being involved in the development of information posted on a server.

The Web offers a tremendous potential to build virtual communities. With it, large and complex problems which concern us are now not only up to individuals to solve. By means of global networking on the Internet, special interest groups and clubs are being formed. These groups can break down large issues into smaller ones and collaborate to solve problems. Mathematicians, for example, have joined forces to work on large problems via the Internet. These activities have led to new discoveries and solutions.

The notion of learners contacting subject matter experts is being explored in classrooms around the world. This practice reinforces the idea that the classroom teacher need not be the single expert upon which the student has to rely. Students can find experts via the Internet and use e-mail to exchange ideas and opinions. Most of these experts are willing to work with students when approached by e-mail and provided with a structure for exchanging messages. When a student takes all of these resources and combines them, the Internet can become a mechanism for transforming learners into serious writers and publishers.

Engaging students with subject matter experts, or using the Internet as a virtual library, or as a mechanism for visiting virtual museums and exhibitions are all ways the Internet has been explored to date. The World Wide Web can also serve as a vehicle for enhanced content and provide an arena for children to exchange their ideas on complex subjects.

FUTURE PROSPECTS

We will see the development of more authoring tools and imbedded "applets" for use within the World Wide Web. These programs will allow multiple media to run within a single Web page. Readers of Web-based projects will be able to run simulations or models created by the author, even in the absence of specific applications.

The growth of student-based Internet publishing, with the HyperText Markup Language (HTML) and other authoring tools, will assume the learning role begun by HyperCard. Teachers witnessed a tremendous change in student collaboration and learning when their students created reports using HyperCard. With HTML, students can create even more dynamic documents and publish them on the World Wide Web to share with learners around the world. New tools, available soon, will further encourage this creation of dynamic and interactive materials for a global audience.

CONCLUSION

The potential of integrating media, using it to enhance our under-standing of complex issues, and creating meaningful learning environ-ments remains yet to be fully discovered. This is our challenge and our prospect for tomorrow.

ABOUT THE AUTHOR

Kim Rose is on the research staff of Apple Computer's Learning Concepts Group. The Learning Concepts Group explores how new technologies, and media built on them, can enrich learning environments for children and adults. Kim works with a consortium of schools in Southern California to develop collaborative dynamic curricula, accessed through a newly created wide area telecommunications network. Kim can be contacted at Apple Computer Inc., Learning Concepts Group, 131 S. Barrington Place, #200, Los Angeles, CA 90049. (310) 471–7339, fax:(310) 471–2352, e-mail: rose5@applelink.apple.com

Bibliography

This is a partial list of sources we've found helpful as we've begun to learn about the Internet. It is by no means exhaustive or complete. It is meant as a starting point.

BOOKS

Badgett, Tom. *Welcome to . . . The Internet.* New York: MIS Press, 1995. ISBN 1-558-28424-9.

Butler, Mark. *How to Use the Internet.* Emeryville, California: Ziff-Davis Press, 1994. ISBN 1-56276-222-2.

Cady, Glee Harrah and Pat McGregor. *Mastering the Internet.* San Francisco: SYBEX, 1995. ISBN 0-7821-1645-0.

Clark, David. *Student's Guide to the Internet.* Indianapolis, Indiana: Alpha Books, 1995. ISBN 1-56761-545-7.

Comer, Douglas E. *The Internet Book.* Englewood Cliffs, New Jersey: Prentice-Hall, 1995. ISBN 0-131-51565-9.

Cummins, Jim and Dennis Sayers. *Brave New Schools: Challenging Cultural Illiteracy Through Global Learning Networks.* New York: St. Martin's Press, 1995. ISBN 0-312-126697.

December, John and Neil Randall. *The World Wide Web Unleashed.* Indianapolis, Indiana: Sams, 1995. ISBN 0-672-30617-4.

Dern, Daniel P. *Internet Guide for New Users.* New York: McGraw-Hill, 1994. ISBN 0-07-0165106.

Eager, Bill. *The Information Superhighway Illustrated.* Indianapolis, Indiana: Que, 1994. ISBN 1-565-29892-6.

————. *Using the World Wide Web.* Indianapolis, Indiana: Que, 1994. ISBN 0-789-70016-6.

Ellsworth, Jill. *Education on the Internet.* Indianapolis, Indiana: Sams, 1995. ISBN 0-672-30595-X.

Engst, Adam. *Internet Starter Kit for Macintosh.* Indianapolis, Indiana: Que, 1994. ISBN 1-568-30111-1.

Ford, Andrew. *Spinning the World Wide Web: How to Provide Information on the Internet.* London: International Thomas Pub., 1995. ISBN 0-442-01996-3.

Frazier, Deneen. *Internet for Kids.* San Francisco: SYBEX, 1995. ISBN 0-782-11741-4.

Gaffin, Adam. *Everybody's Guide to the Internet.* Cambridge, Massachusetts: MIT Press, 1994. ISBN 0-262-57105-6.

Gale Guide to Internet Databases. Detroit: Gale Research, 1995. ISBN 0-7876-01985.

Gilster, Paul. *Finding It on the Internet: The Internet Navigator's Guide to Search Tools & Techniques.* New York: Wiley, 1996. ISBN 0-471-12695-0.

Grossbrenner, Alfred. *The Little Online Book.* Berkeley, California: Peachpit Press, 1995. ISBN 1-566-09130-6.

Hahn, Harley and Rick Stout. *The Internet Yellow Pages.* Berkeley, California: Osborne McGraw-Hill, 1995. ISBN 0-07-8820987.

John, Nancy R. and Edward J. Valauskas. *The Internet Troubleshooter: Help for the Logged-On and Lost.* Chicago: ALA Press, 1994. ISBN 0-838-90633-8.

Joseph, Linda. *World Link: An Internet Guide for Educators, Parents and Students.* Columbus, Ohio: Greydon Press, 1995. ISBN 1-57074-244-8.

Krol, Ed. *The Whole Internet User's Guide & Catalog.* Sebastapol, California: O'Reilly & Associates, 1994. ISBN 1-565-92063-5.

McClure, Charles and William E. Moen. *Libraries and the Internet/ NREN: Perspectives, Issues and Challenges.* Westport, Connecticut: Meckler, 1994. ISBN 0-88736-8247.

Otte, Peter. *The Information Superhighway: Beyond the Internet.* Indianapolis, Indiana: Que, 1994. ISBN 1-565-29825-X.

Randall, Neil. *Teach Yourself the Internet: Around the World in 21 Days.* Indianapolis, Indiana: Sams, 1995. ISBN 1-672-30735-9.

Valauskas, Edward J. and Nancy R. John. *The Internet Initiative: Libraries Providing Internet Services and How They Plan, Pay, and Manage.* Chicago: ALA Press, 1995. ISBN 0-838-90668-0.

Wiggins, Richard. *The Internet for Everyone: A Guide for Users and Providers.* New York: McGraw-Hill, 1995. ISBN 0-070-67019-6.

JOURNALS AND NEWSLETTERS

Internet Homesteader
ISSN 1076-4143
State University of New York
SUNY/OCLC Network and Office of Library Services
SUNY Plaza
Albany, NY 12246
(518) 443-5444

Internet Letter: On Corporate Users, Internetworking & Information Services
ISSN 1070-9851
1294 National Press Building
Washington, DC 20045
(202) 638-6036
http://222.infohaus.com/access/by-seller/Internet_Letter

Internet Research: Electronic Networking Applications and Policy
ISSN 1066-2243
MCB University Press Ltd.
60/62 Toller Lane
Bradford, West Yorkshire
England BD8 9BY
Phone: 44 1274 777700

Internet Week: News and Analysis of Internet Business Opportunities
ISSN 1081-2474
1201 Seven Locks Road
Potomac, MD 20854-2931
(301) 309-3847
http://www.phillips.com/pbi/iw

Internet World: The Magazine for Internet Users
ISSN 0164-3923
20 Ketchum Street
Westport, CT 06880
Internet e-mail: info@mecklermedia.com

NetGuide: The Guide to the Internet and Online Services
ISSN 1078-4632
CMP Media
600 Community Drive
Manhasset, NY 11030
(800) 829-0421
http://techweb.cmp.com/net

NetTeach News
ISSN 10570-2954
13102 Weather Vane Way
Herndon, VA 22071-2944
Phone: (703) 471-0593
Internet: netteach@chaos.com
This newsletter focuses on the use of educational networking.

Wired
ISSN 1059-1028
520 Third St.
San Francisco, CA 94107
(415) 222–6200
Internet email: info@wired.com

VIDEOS AND OTHER RESOURCES

Connecting to the Future
NASA CORE
Lorain County Joint Vocational School
15181 Route 58 South
Oberlin, OH 44074
Phone: (216) 774-1051 x 293/294
Fax: (216) 774-2144
This video provides guidance for schools considering Internet connectivity.

Global Quest: Internet in the Classroom
NASA CORE
Lorain County Joint Vocational School
15181 Route 58 South
Oberlin, OH 44074
Phone: (216) 774-1051 x 293/294
Fax: (216) 774-2144
This video shares the benefits of Internet use in the classroom. It describes why the Internet is an amazing school resource.

Internet Sites Mentioned in this Book

Note: This appendix does not itemize all of the LISTSERVs and newsgroups mentioned. The editors have verified all sites as of January 1996.

Apple Computer Internet Server Home Page
http://www.solutions.apple.com/internet/default.html

Arbor Height's Cool Writers' Magazine
http://www.halcyon.com/ahcool/home.html

Arbor Heights Elementary School, Seattle, Washington
http://www.halcyon.com/arborhts/arborhts.html

Baby Maiasaura in Berkeley
http://ucmp1.berkeley.edu/diapsids/ornithischia/hadrosauria.html

Badger Gopher
gopher://badger.state.wi.us/

Beginner's Guide to HTML
http://www.ncsa.uiuc.edu/demoweb/html-primer.html

Belleville School District, Wisconsin
http://joe.uwex.edu/~k12/Belleville/index.html

Bethel High School, Virginia
http://www.bethel.hampton.k12.va.us/

Boulder Valley Internet Project
http://bvsd.k12.co.us

CedarNet, a FreeNet in the Cedar River Valley of northeast Iowa
http://www.CedarNet.org

ChemViz
http://www.ncsa.uiuc.edu/edu/ChemViz/

CIA World Factbook
http://www.odci.gov/cia/publications/95fact/index.html

Classroom Connect
http://www.wentworth.com/classroom/edulinks.htm

Community Newspaper
http://www.nueva.pvt.k12.ca.us/pipe/pipe.newspaper.html

Cool Color Tool
http://firehorse.com/colorhex

Dino Russ's Lair, the Earthnet Info Server
http://128.174.172.76:/isgsroot/dinos/dinos_home.html

Evaluating the Environment
http://cotf.edu/ETE/etehome.html

Field Guide to the Mudflats of San Francisco Bay
http://www.nueva.pvt.k12.ca.us/pipe/pipe.mudguide.html

Franklin Museum of Virtual Science
http://sln.fi.edu/

From DNA to Dinosaurs, Field Museum of Natural History
http://www.bvis.uic.edu/museum/ Dna_To_Dinosaurs.html

Global School Network
http://gsn.org/gsn/gsn.projects.html

Global Show-n-Tell
http://emma.manymedia.com:80/show-n-tell/

Grateful Dead
http://www.uccs.edu/~ddodd/gdhome.html

Happy Valley School, Santa Cruz, California
http://www.happy-valley.hvsd.k12.ca.us

Highland Park Elementary School, Austin, Texas
http://www.hipark.austin.isd.tenet.edu/home/main.html

HyperCard reference stack on dinosaurs
http://152.30.18.100/Documentation/Dinosaurs.hqx

Internet Starter Kit
http://www.mcp.com/hayden/iskm/

Kaukauna Electra Quinney Middle School, Wisconsin
http://athenet.net/~joker/

Learning Through Collaborative Visualization Project, Northwestern
University
http://www.covis.nwu.edu/

LISTSERVs for K-12 education
http://www.asd.k12.ak.us/EdLISTSERVS.html

MacHTTP, StarNine Technologies
http://www.biap.com/machttp/machttp_software.html

Madison, Wisconsin Middle School 2000
http://198.150.8.9/

Marshfield, Wisconsin School District
http://www.uscyber.com/education/marshfield-k12/

Meet the Spiders
http://pebbles.pluggedin.org/summer_projects_1995/spiders/
meetthespiders/meetthespiders.html

MidLink Magazine, Discovery Middle School, Orlando, Florida
http://longwood.cs.ucf.edu/~MidLink

Millard Public Schools, Omaha, Nebraska
http://esu3.esu3.k12.ne.us/districts/millard/mps/

Museum of Paleontology, University of California at Berkeley
http://ucmp1.berkeley.edu/ exhibittext/dinosaur.html

NASA's StarChild Project
http://guinan.gsfc.nasa.gov/K12/Proposal.html

NOAA's El Nino page
http://www.pmel.noaa.gov/toga-tao/el-nino/home.html

Nueva School, Hillsborough, California
http://www.nueva.pvt.k12.ca.us

Bill Nye, the Science Guy
http://www.seanet.com/Vendors/billnye/nyelabs.html

Ocean Planet
http://seawifs.gsfc.nasa.gov/ocean_planet.html

Ray Olszewski
http://www.nueva.pvt.k12.ca.us/~ray/

Plugged In
http://www.pluggedin.org/
http://pebbles.pluggedin.org/pie/piehome.html

Private School Resource
http://www.brigadoon.com:80/psrnet/index.html

Rain Forest Workshop
http://mh.osd.wednet.edu/

Royal Tyrrell Museum of Paleontology
http://www.tyrrell.com/

St. Philomena School, Des Moines, Washington
http://www.halcyon.com/dale/stphil.html

Science and Math Initiatives (SAMI)
http://www.c3.lanl.gov/~jspeck/SAMI-home.html

Stephen's watercolor
http://emma.manymedia.com:80/show-n-tell/stephen2.gif

Taking Stock
http://www.santacruz.k12.ca.us/~jpost/projects/TS/TS.html

Texas Rivers Project, First Colony Middle School, Sugarland, Texas
http://chico.rice.edu/armadillo/Ftbend/rivers.html

Uncle Bob's Kid's Page
http://gagme.wwa.com/~bob/kids.html

Virtual Field Trips of Monterey Bay
http://www.santacruz.k12.ca.us/~jpost/vft/

Vocal Point
http://bvsd.k12.co.us/schools/cent/Newspaper/Newspaper.html

Volcano World
http://volcano.und.nodak.edu/vw.html

Washington High School, part of the Milwaukee, Wisconsin Public Schools
gopher://whscdp.whs.edu:70/1

Web Weaver
http://www.northnet.org/best/Web.Weaver/WW.html

Web66: International WWW School Registry
http://web66.coled.umn.edu/schools.html

Wisconsin Department of Public Instruction
http://www.state.wi.us/agencies/dpi

Interesting Web Sites

GENERAL DIRECTORIES AND INDICES:

Gopher Jewels
http://galaxy.einet.net/GJ/index.html
Gopher Jewels catalogs many of the best Gopher sites by categories (subject tree) and takes you to the relevant information.

Lycos
http://www.lycos.com/
Lycos provides a huge catalog of documents on the Internet, including an easy-to-use way to search that catalog. Their "Education" section is a rich resource.

WebCrawler
http://webcrawler.com/
The WebCrawler is a search tool to help you locate information on the Internet. The WebCrawler is operated by America Online, Inc. at their Web Studios in San Francisco, CA.

Yahoo!
http://www.yahoo.com
Yahoo! is a hierarchical subject-oriented guide for the World Wide Web and Internet. Yahoo! lists sites and categorizes them into appropriate subject categories. Of special interest, check out their category "Education."

GENERAL EDUCATION LOCATION SITES:

Web 66
http://web66.coled.umn.edu/
The Web66 project is designed to facilitate the introduction of this technology into K12 schools. The goals of this project are: 1.To help K12 educators learn how to set up their own Internet servers; 2.To link K12 WWW servers and the educators and students at those schools; 3.To help K12 educators find and use K12 appropriate resources on the WWW. This site contains one of the most comprehensive lists of schools on the Internet.

CURRICULUM:

Eisenhower National Clearinghouse
http://www.enc.org/
   The Eisenhower National Clearinghouse is designed to help educators improve teaching and learning in science and mathematics education.

WebEd Curriculum Links
http://badger.state.wi.us/agencies/dpi/www/WebEd.html
   The WebEd K12 Curriculum Links has been under construction since 1993. It contains networked information which would support curriculum in a local school district.

OTHER INTERESTING SITES:

Apple Education News
http://www.info.apple.com/education/
   Serving preschools through high schools located in the United States, Apple Education presents calendars of teacher training events, Apple research reports in the Classroom of Tomorrow series, products of special interest to educators, and resources to raise awareness of Apple's commitment to information technology for schools.

Busy Teachers WebSite K-12
http://www.gatech.edu/lcc/idt/Students/Cole/Proj/K-12/K12wel.html
   This site is designed to provide teachers with direct source materials, lesson plans and classroom activities with a minimum of site-to-site linking, and to provide an enjoyable and rewarding experience for the teacher who is learning to use the Internet.

CyberFair 96: Share & Unite
http://www.gsn.org/gsn/cfhome.html
   Building on the global Internet platform, International Schools CyberFair 96 participants will effectively create curricular content for use by students around the world through cooperation, mutual discovery, and content creation. Participating schools will be asked to conduct a research project involving community resources and publish their project on the Internet's World Wide Web.

Cyber High School
http://www.webcom.com/~cyberhi/
   Cyber High School is the first high school that is entirely resi-

dent on the Internet. It offers a complete curriculum and instruction and is accessible to anyone who has Internet access, anywhere in the world.

Global SchoolNet Foundation
http://gsn.org/
Since 1985 Global SchoolNet Foundation has been a leader in the instructional applications of telecommunications. Today the Global SchoolNet Foundation, a non-profit corporation, is a major contributor to the philosophy, design, culture, and content of educational networking on the Internet and in the classroom.

I°EARN
http://www.igc.apc.org/iearn/
I°EARN empowers teachers and young people (ages 6-19) to work together in different parts of the world at very low cost through a global telecommunications network. The purpose of I°EARN is to enable participants to undertake projects designed to make a meaningful difference in the health and welfare of the planet and its people. I°EARN is a non-profit organization. I°EARN is expanding to additional international sites daily and now includes over 500 schools in more than twenty countries.

ICONnect
http://ericir.syr.edu/ICONN/ihome.html
ICONnect offers school library media specialists, teachers, and students the opportunity to learn the skills necessary to navigate the information superhighway through online courses, curriculum advisors, mini-grants and an interactive question and answer service. ICONnect is sponsored by the American Association of School Librarians.

KidLink: Global Networking for Youth
http://global.kidlink.org/home-txt.html
KIDS-96 is a grassroots project aimed at getting as many children in the age group 10 -15 a possible involved in a GLOBAL dialog.

PBS Online
http://www.pbs.org/
The PBS home page is designed to provide easy access to information related to public television. This site also includes learning services and connections to other educational sites.

UEweb

http://eric-web.tc.columbia.edu/

UEweb offers manuals, brief articles, annotated bibliographies, reviews, and summaries of outstanding publications, and conference announcements in urban education. Many items in UEweb are published by the ERIC Clearinghouse on Urban Education and are available for free or a nominal charge, as described in its publication list. If you have documents you would like to submit to ERIC/CUE see the call for documents for sending instructions. UEweb is presented by the ERIC Clearinghouse on Urban Education (ERIC/CUE) and is funded by the U.S. Department of Education, Office of Education Research and Improvement.

SPECIFIC DISCIPLINES

Art

Museums

Los Angeles County Museum of Art
http://www.lacma.org/
Palmer Museum of Art, Penn State University
http://cac.psu.edu/~mtd120/palmer/
WebMuseum, Paris
http://mistral.enst.fr/wm/net/
World Art Treasures
http://sgwww.epfl.ch/BERGER/index.html

Specific artists and exhibits

Age of Enlightenment in French art
http://dmf.culture.fr/files/imaginary_exhibition.html
Ansel Adams
http://bookweb.cwis.uci.edu:8042/AdamsHome.html
ArtMap
http://www.anima.wis.net//ARTWORLDhome.html
@Art Gallery
http://gertrude.art.uiuc.edu/@art/gallery.html
Art on the Net
http://www.art.net/
Cezanne
http://www.cezanne.com/

French cave paintings
http://www.culture.fr/culture/gvpda-en.htm
Leonardo da Vinci Museum
http://cellini.leonardo.net/museum/main.html
Musees de Paris
http://meteora.ucsd.edu/~norman/paris/Musees/
Treasures of the Czars
http://www.times.st-pete.fl.us/Treasures/Default.html
Jan Vermeer
http://www.ccsf.caltech.edu/~roy/vermeer/
World of Escher
http://www.texas.net/escher/

English

General

Children's Literature Web Guide
http://www.ucalgary.ca/~dkbrown/index.html
Linkoping Science Fiction and Fantasy Archive
http://www.lysator.liu.se/sf_archive/
Quotations Page
http://www.xmission.com/~mgm/quotes/

Specific Authors

Henry V
http://sec-look.uiowa.edu/henry/
Lewis Carroll
http://www.students.uiuc.edu/~jbirenba/carroll.html
The Two Towers
http://www.servtech.com/staff/stisa/towers/index.html

Writing

KidPub WWW Publishing
http://www.en-garde.com/kidpub/

For Teachers Only: Education Resources

Academy for Educational Development
http://www.aed.org
At-Risk Institute
http://www.ed.gov/prog_info/At-Risk/

Berit's Best Sites for Children
   http://www.cochran.com/theosite/ksites.html
CACI: Children Accessing Controversial Information
   http://www.zen.org/~brendan/caci.html
Homework Page
   http://www.tpoint.net/~jewels/homework.html
Kids Web
   http://www.npac.syr.edu/textbook/kidsweb/
McNair Scholars Program, San Diego State University
   http://sonofsun.sdsu.edu/usp/mcnair/
Teacher Talk
   http://education.indiana.edu/cas/tt/tthmpg.html
U.S. Department of Education, Division of Adult Education and
Literacy's (DAEL) information network
   gopher://gopher.dial-in.nw.dc.us
Urban Education Web
   http://eric-web.tc.columbia.edu
Utah Education Network
   gopher://gopher.uen.org
Western Interstate Commission for Higher Education
   http://www.wiche.edu

Foreign Languages

General

Foreign Languages and Cultures Center
   http://www.speakeasy.org/~dbrick/Hot/foreign.html
Human Languages Page
   http://www.willamette.edu/~tjones/Language-Page.html

French

Les Reunions Francophones de Chicago
   http://www.physio.nwu.edu/~ray/reunions.html
LIBERATION, a French daily newspaper
   http://www.netfrance.com/Libe/
Web French lessons
   http://teleglobe.ca/~leo/french.html

Geography

General

The Great Adventure, Children's Museum of the Canadian Museum of Civilization http://www.cmcc.muse.digital.ca/cmc/cmceng/cmeng.html

Africa

Ethiopia
http://rs6.loc.gov/et_00_00.html#_05_04
Ghana
http://www.uta.fi/~csfraw/ghana.html
University of Wisconsin, African studies
http://www.wisc.edu/afr
ZAMNET, the Zambian National Gopher
gopher://gopher.unza.zm

Arctic

Arctic Circle Web
http://spirit.lib.uconn.edu/ArcticCircle

Asia

China News
http://www.hk.net/~drummond/milesj/china.html
India Network
http://india.bgsu.edu/index.html
Tokyo!
http://shrine.cyber.ad.jp/~repka/main.html

Middle East

Saudi Arabia
http://www.rahul.net/abadi/saudi1.html

North America

Cuba Web
http://www.unipr.it/~davide/cuba/home.html
New Orleans, Louisiana
http://www.geopages.com/SunsetStrip/1202/
Pennsylvania Dutch Country
http://www.welcome.com

History

General

National Center for Preservation Technology and Training
gopher://gopher.ncptt.nps.gov

Gateway to World History
http://neal.ctstateu.edu/history/world_history/world_history.html

American history

Adventures of Wells Fargo
http://wellsfargo.com/ftr/ftrsty/
American Memory, Library of Congress
http://rs6.loc.gov/amhome.html/
Henry Ford Museum
http://hfm.umd.umich.edu/
Virtual Riverboat
http://www.acy.digex.net/~capnmark/home.html

Mathematics

General

Center for Science and Mathematics Education
http://www.fys.ruu.nl/~csmeut/
Education
http://www.enc.org
Eisenhower National Clearinghouse for Mathematics and Science
History of Mathematics
http://aleph0.clarku.edu/~djoyce/mathhist/mathhist.html
Mathematical Quotations
http://math.furman.edu/~mwoodard/mquot.html
Mathematicians of the Day
http://www-groups.dcs.st-and.ac.uk/~history/Day_files/Now.html
Mathematics education
http://www-hpcc.astro.washington.edu/scied/math.html
Mathematics Lesson Plans
http://www.cs.rice.edu/~sboone/Lessons/lptitle.html
National Teachers Enhancement Network
http://www.montana.edu/~wwwxs/
Women Mathematicians
http://www.scottlan.edu/lriddle/women/women.htm

Geometry and Other Subjects

Calculus & Mathematica
http://www-cm.math.uiuc.edu/
Geometry Center
http://www.geom.umn.edu/

MathMagic
http://forum.swarthmore.edu:80/mathmagic/

Science

General

Lawrence Berkeley Laboratory's Ethical, Legal, and Social Issues
in Science Web
http://www.lbl.gov/Education/ELSI/ELSI.html

Agriculture

Minnesota Extension Service
gopher://gopher.mes.umn.edu
Progressive Farmer
http://www.pathfinder.com/@@JX@ENHA1lAMAQGQa/PF/
index.html

Biology

NetFrog
http://curry.edschool.virginia.edu/~insttech/frog/

Chemistry

Periodic Table of the Elements
http://www-c8.lanl.gov/infosys/html/periodic/periodic-main.html
Poly-Links
http://www.polymers.com/

Environment

Institute for the Environment
http://www.gwu.edu/~greenu/
Natural Resources Defense Council
http://www.nrdc.org/nrdc
U.S. Department of Agriculture, Natural Resources Conservation
Service
http://www.ncg.nrcs.usda.gov/

Natural History

Electronic Prehistoric Shark Museum
http://turnpike.net/emporium/C/celestial/epsm.htm

Nutrition

The Nutrition Expert
http://www.alaska.net:80/~tne

Oceanography

Birch Aquarium-Museum, Scripps Institution of Oceanography
http://aqua.ucsd.edu/

Physics

Albert Einstein Online
http://www.sas.upenn.edu/~smfriedm/einstein.html
Fermi National Accelerator Laboratory Education Office
http://www-ed.fnal.gov/

Space Sciences

NASA K-12 Internet Initiative
http://quest.arc.nasa.gov/

Weather

Hurricane Felix
http://www.netcreations.com/hurricane/
WeatherNet
http://cirrus.sprl.umich.edu/wxnet

Index

A

Abilock, Debbie, 83
Ahlness, Mark, 25
Apple Computer, Learning
    Concepts Group, 196-203
Apple LocalTalk, 76
AppleWorks, use of, 28
Area Education Agency (Cedar
    Falls, Iowa),
    Internet activities at, 159-167
Asahi, 152

B

BadgerDial (Wisconsin project),
    69-70
Banks, Steve, 25
Beasley, Dale E., 23-33
Beebe, Paul, 182
Bell, David, 107-116
BellSouth Business Systems, 173
Best, Robert, 24
Bibliography on the Internet,
    205-208
Black, Libby, 147-158
Boulder Valley Internet Project
    (Colorado),
    Internet activities at, 147-158
Boulder Valley School District
    (Colorado),
    Internet activities at, 89-95
Building models, 54-104
Burns, Marilyn, 142

C

California Educational Initia-
    tives Fund, 136, 140
California Technology Grants,
    136
Catholic school
    early Internet activity at, 23-
    33
CedarNet, 163-164
Centennial Middle School
    (Boulder, Colorado),
    Internet activities at, 147-158
Champaign (Illinois) public
    schools
    Internet activities at, 35-42
Chat rooms, 137
Chat servers, ban on, 122
Chemistry, relation to the
    Internet, 38-40
ChemViz, relation to the Inter-
    net, 38-39
Children's features on the Web,
    11-12
Children's Museum (Raleigh,
    North Carolina), 173
Christa McAuliffe Fellowship
    Award, 136
Christopher Newport University,
    100
Clauset, Tom, 129
Colgan, Matt, 155
Collegiality, 138

Community leaders
support from 189
Computer literacy
nature of, 198-199
Connectivity access, 47-48, 90-91
Continuous training, 20
Crawford, Cindy, 77-78
Curriculum improvements with global projects, 127-134
Curriculum planning, integrating the Internet with, 19, 105-144

D

Department of Information Technology (DoIT)(University of Wisconsin), 67-68
Distance learning, rethinking, 198
Dixon, Scott, 147-158
Donlan, Leni, 138

E

E-mail, limitations on, 122-123
Educational activities on the Internet, Hampton City (Virginia) Schools, 100-103
Educational Service Units (ESUs)(Nebraska), 44
ElderNet, role of, 81
Electronic mail, 122-123
Electronic pen pals, 136-137
Elementary School Internet projects (Nebraska), 59-62
Enloe Magnet High School (Raleigh, North Carolina), 173
Ertel, Monica, 233

Ethernet, local area network (LAN), 48
wired with Apple LocalTalk, 76
Eudora, 82, 121
Exploratorium Center for Teaching and Learning (San Francisco), 7-9

F

Fagnant, Christa, 130
Falanga, Rosemarie E., 3-14
Family Tree-Mail project, 131-132
Fantasies, two stories on Internet's effect on children, 3-14
Fetch, 82
Fieldtrips, 132
Fisher, Wayne, 43-51
Free-Nets, 163
French Connection, 58
Future directions, 124-125
Future projects, 142-143

G

General Telephone Company, Wisconsin grants from, 71
Geogame, 129-131
Gifted and Talented Education Grants, 136
Ginsberg-Jaeckle, Matthew, 155
Global SchoolHouse, Jefferson Junior High School (Oceanside, California), 131-132
Global SchoolNet Foundation (El Cajon, California), 127-134
Global Show-n-Tell, 7
Gopher, use of, 69, 77-80, 82

H

Hampton City (Virginia) Schools
Internet activities at, 97-104
Hanley, Denny, 61
Happy Valley School (Santa
Cruz, California), Internet
activities at, 135-144
Hardenbergh, Kathy, 58
Hardware and software up-
grades, 79-81
Hobbs, Offie, 182
Home pages
call for participation in, 175-
176
collaboration in creating, 172-
173
contents of, 163, 171-172
creation of, 23-33, 124, 142,
169-179, 184
guidelines for success, 173-
175
using participants, 176-178
Hurwitz, Sharon, 102
HyperStudio, 36-37, 141
HyperText Markup Language
(HTML), 24
use of in student publications,
151

I

Individualized learning philoso-
phy, 119-120
Infrastructure and staffing,
Hampton City (Virginia)
Schools, 98-99
Integrating the Internet with
curriculum, 105-144
International communication
school children involved in,
129

Internet, effects of on children,
two scenarios, 3-14
Internet access, Hampton City
(Virginia) Schools, 99-100
Internet activities
future prospects for, 201
pitfalls of, 197
significance of, 196-202
Internet programs
Omaha Public Schools
(Nebraska), 15-21
Internet prospects for tomorrow,
196-202
Internet sites mentioned in this
book, 209-213
Internet teaching, rules for, 107-
116

J

Jacobsen, Donald E., 55-64
Jacobson, Russ, 11
Jensen, Curtis, 159-167

K

Kalmon, Stevan, 117-126
Keithly, John, 24
Kidsphere, 175-176
Kimura, Marilyn, 83
Knight-Ridder Information
Design Laboratory, 149
Knyffeler, Kay, 58

L

Landis, Melodee, 46
Landweber, Larry, 182
Learning arrangements and
techniques, 120-122
Learning Through Collaborative
Visualization (CoVis)
Project at Northwestern
University, 8

Lee, Michael, 184
Library and Information Services Exploratorium (San Francisco)
 role of, 3-14
Ligon GT Magnet Middle School (Raleigh, North Carolina)
 Internet activities at, 169-179
Linux, 76
LISTSERVs, 80, 81
 participation in, 27
 use of for home pages, 176
Little, Nina, 15-21
Lohr, Neah J., 65-74
Louisville Junior High School (Louisville, Nebraska), 107-116

M

Madison Academic Computing Center (MACC), 67
Madison Metropolitan School District (Madison, Wisconsin), Internet activities at, 182-191
Madison Middle School 2000 (MMS 2000) (Madison, Wisconsin), Internet activities at, 182-191
Massachusetts Institute of Technology, Advanced Math and Physics Help Desk, 57
Mathison, Kathy Jo, 174
McCann, Jack, 25
McCullen, Caroline, 25, 169-179
Meaningful learning, nature of, 199-200
Middle school students, Internet activities for, 182-191

Millard Public Schools (Nebraska)
 Internet activities at, 55-64
Moore, Jane, 130
Moran, Juan, 38
Mosaic
 use of, 25, 39, 124
Multi-User Domains (MUD), ban on, 122
Murata, Shigefumi, 152

N

National Center for Atmospheric Research, 149,150
National Center for Supercomputing Applications (NCSA), 38
National Science Foundation, 8, 150-151
Nebraska
 Internet activities at, 55-64
 Internet history of, 44-46
Nebraska Department of Education, 43-51
Nebraska Education Network (NEnet)
 development of, 44
Nebraska network
 benefits of, 18-20, 49
 design of, 49-50
 prospects for, 50
Netscape, use of on home pages, 25, 82, 124
Networking, relation to education in Champaign (Illinois), 39-41
Networks, formation of Omaha (Nebraska) public schools, 19
New Vista High School (Boulder, Colorado
 Internet activities at, 117-126

Newsday project, 131
Newspapers, student, 82, 131, 147-158
Norris, George, 60
North Central Regional Education Laboratory (NCREL), publicity given by, 188
Nueva School (California)
early activities at, 76-78
future challenges to, 83-84
Internet activities at, 75-87
Nueva School (California)
lessons to be learned, 84-85
Nueva School (California), projects carried out at, 82-83

O
Olszewski, Ray, 75-87
Omaha (Nebraska) Public Schools, Internet activities at, 15-21

P
Pacific Bell, 136
Pacific Bell's California Research and Education Network (CalREN)
use of PIPE, 79
PageMaker, 119
Parents, need for involvement of in the Internet, 5-7
Pasos, Lorna, 127-134
PBS Special
publicity given by, 188
Peninsula Internet Partners in Education (PIPE), 78-79, 81-82
Pine, 121
PIPE. See Peninsula Internet Partners in Education (PIPE)

Plugged In, 8, 9
Post, Jory, 135-144
Publishing on the Web, 145-191

R
Red Planet Project, 58
Research projects
value and limitations discovered, 123-124
Rogers, Al, 128
Rose, Kim, 196-203
Rosenbloom, Jay, 182
Rowe, Barry E., 35-42
Rural area connections
Boulder Valley (Colorado) Project, 91-93

S
Sabelli, Dr. Nora, 38
Sachter, Randy, 94
SAMI database. *See Science and Math Initiatives database.*
School Instructional Information Managers
role of, 15-21
Science and Math Initiatives (SAMI) database, Boulder Valley (Colorado) Project, 93
Sciences
high school Internet activities involved with, 35-42
Secondary and Middle School Internet projects (Nebraska), 56-59
Servers
rise of in student publications, 165-166
Skinner, Steve, 56
Soglin, Mayor Paul, 189
Speckien, John R., 89-95

Spitz, Barbara, 182-191
St. Margaret-Mary School
    (Chicago, Illinois), 137
St. Philomena School (Des
    Moines, Washington),
    Internet activities at, 23-33
Stallard, Charles, 97-104
Stallard, Mary, 102-103
Statewide (Nebraska) preK-12
    model, Internet connectiv-
    ity, 43-51
Stock market projects, 139-140
Student publications, 147-158,
    159-167, 186-188
    purpose of, 160-161
    requirements for, 164-165
Suburban K-12 public school
    district (Nebraska)
    Internet networks at, 55-64
Tarabochia, Karen, 26

T
Teachers
    importance of Internet
        projects to, 190
    involvement with the Inter-
        net, 7-8
Teaching techniques, 107-116
    importance of fast equipment,
        109
    importance of time, 109
    instructors' need to relax in
        classroom, 114
    learning from mistakes, 113-
        114
    LISTSERV postings, 112-113
    need for close supervision,
        110
    simplicity needed in lessons,
        114
    student knowledge of teach-
        ing goals, 108

    use of LISTSERVs, 110-112
Telecommunications, Nebraska,
    efforts involving, 43-51
Telecomputing in Smart Schools,
    97-104
Texas Rivers Project, 174
Thompson, Governor Tommy,
    70
    support of school efforts by,
        187-188
TOWS: The Online Write Stuff,
    140
Toyota Tapestry Grant, 57
Tucker, Jill, 151

U
University of Colorado School of
    Journalism, 149
University of Wisconsin (Madi-
    son), 67-68
UNIX, 165
USA Today, 189

V
Valauskas, Edward, 233
Vanandel, Joe, 150
Veronica, 78, 123
Virginia Department of
    Education's Electronic
    Network (VAPEN), 100
Vocal Point, 151-157
    process for, 155-157
    student-run online newspa-
        per, 147-158
Vraniak, Tara, 183

W
Wagner, Roger, 36
WAIS, 123
WAN/LAN Committee, Omaha
    Public Schools, 19
Web. See World Wide Web

Wide area network (WAN),
    Nebraska, 48
Wilhoyte, Cheryl, 187, 189·
Williams, Roger, 128-129
WISCNet (Wisconsin Education
    Network), 66-68
Wisconsin, biennial budget of, 71
Wisconsin public schools
    communication in, history of,
    66-67
    Internet access and curricular
    use in, 65-74
    Internet plan for and status,
    68-69
Wisconsin Public Service Com-
    mission (PSC), 70-71

Wisconsin State Agency Internet
    Gopher, 69
Wisconsin Telecommunications
    Act, 70-71
Withem, Senator Ron, 46
World Wide Web
    browsers, Mosaic and
    Netscape, 124
    home pages, creation of, 24-
    29
    news gathering using, 141
    significance of, 200-201
    sites, list of those of interest,
    215-224
Writing and publishing online,
    140

About the Editors

Edward J. Valauskas is founder and Principal of Internet Mechanics, a consulting group providing assistance on the Internet to Schools, libraries, corporations, and non-profit associations. He has co-authored and co-edited several books including *Macintoshed Libraries* (Apple Library Users Group, 1987–1994), *Internet Troubleshooter* (ALA Editions, 1994), and *Internet Initiatives* (ALA Editions, 1995).

Monica Ertel is Director of Knowledge Systems for Apple Computer, Inc. where she is responsible for investigating new technologies for rich access to information. She is co-editor of *Automated Systems for Access to Multilingual and Multiscript Library Materials* (K.G. Saur, 1994) and author of numerous articles on the use of technology in libraries. She was hired by Apple Computer in 1981 to establish their corporate library. She is also founder of the Apple Library Users Group and is editor-in-chief of its quarterly newsletter.

Other Titles of Interest in the *Neal-Schuman NetGuide Series*